SHIPSHAPE AND BRISTOL FASHION

A Sailor's Guide to Cruising in Comfort and Safety

By
Loren R. Borland
With Drawings by the Auth

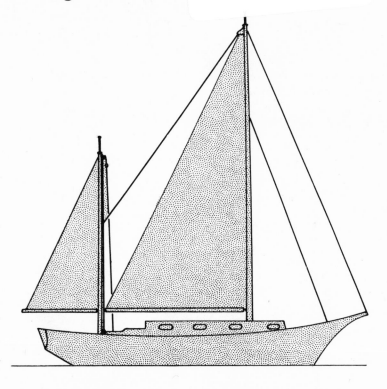

VNR VAN NOSTRAND REINHOLD COMPANY
New York   Cincinnati   Toronto   London   Melbourne

Printed in the United States of America

Published by Van Nostrand Reinhold Company
A division of Litton Educational Publishing, Inc.
135 West 50th Street, New York, NY 10020, U.S.A.

Van Nostrand Reinhold Limited
1410 Birchmount Road
Scarborough, Ontario M1P 2E7, Canada

Van Nostrand Reinhold Australia Pty. Ltd.
17 Queen Street
Mitcham, Victoria 3132, Australia

Van Nostrand Reinhold Company Limited
Molly Millars Lane
Wokingham, Berkshire, England

16 15 14 13 12 11 10 9 8 7 6 5 4 3 2

To David,

without whom this book could not have been written,

and

To Lesley,

with whom it was.

Contents

Introduction

For as long as I can remember, I have loved boats. As a small boy, I repeatedly horrified my mother by my exploits with improvised rafts and other "craft" which I constructed from anything I could find that would float. My creations often fell short of even that simple requirement, and my poor mother's concern for my survival was often rivaled by her exasperation at my muddy clothing and waterlogged shoes. My only and inevitably unconvincing argument was that I could swim and that I hadn't drowned yet.

In the years that have followed, I have tried every kind of boating that has been available to me. From canoeing and canoe sailing to outboard cruising and fishing on lakes and rivers. From week-end dinghy sailing and ocean racing to extended deep-water cruising and chartering and a period during which I lived for a year and a half aboard a thirty-eight foot cutter. I can look back on a varied and amazingly undistinguished yachting career with the satisfaction of having enjoyed some aspects of every kind of boating I have tried, and of having learned a good deal from the almost endless succession of mistakes I have made.

At the very least, I have learned that my real interest lies in cruising. For one thing, I'm getting a little too old to enjoy hiking out in a dinghy on a cold wet day, or driving an ocean racer to the limit of her crew's and rig's endurance. I'd rather shorten sail, heave to and spend the afternoon with a good book when the going gets rough, but that is only part of my reason for preferring cruising to racing.

Cruising, especially deep-water cruising, seems to me to be a little closer to basic reality. There isn't any prescribed course to sail—the cruising skipper sets his own. He enjoys entering a good day's run in the log, but the real premium is on good seamanship and not on speed. There is no racing fleet or committee boat to pick him up if he drives his boat too hard and the rig carries away. He's on his own from the time he sets sail until he drops anchor again, and I suppose this is the deepest source of satisfaction for the cruising man.

This results in an outlook that is a little different from that of the confirmed racing skipper. The cruising man is interested in dependability at all costs, and his rig and equipment reflect this. A little extra weight or windage is not unacceptable if it means absolute reliability. Ground tackle is selected to hold securely in the worst conceivable conditions, and rigging is arranged to permit easy and positive sail handling in the worst sea conditions, and by a crew which is usually well below racing strength.

What I know about cruising has been learned almost exclusively from two sources; good books, and a tremendous number of mistakes. Of these two possibilities, I can heartily recommend learning from books, especially if it means avoiding some of the mistakes. The ideas presented in this book have all been tried and proven under actual cruising conditions. Most of these are items which I have used myself with great satisfaction. The others have been vouched for by yachtsmen whose opinions I respect. In general these items fall into three categories.

The first category is concerned with safety, and I think this should be the first concern of every cruising skipper. By all means require your crew to wear life jackets and safety lines when conditions call for them, but this is not enough. You can also arrange your rigging equipment in such a way that the necessary sail and ship handling can be done without exposing your crew to unnecessary danger.

Second, there is a group of suggestions which are intended to make your cruising more comfortable. I am a great believer in comfort, and can't see the point of not being comfortable when one has a choice. Moreover, even a shorthanded crew that has had plenty of rest and good food can cope with almost anything when the need arises.

Then there is a third group of ideas which are intended to save time. The cruising skipper usually has a whole list of responsibilities, any one of which might be a full time assignment in an ocean racing crew. The navigation has to be accurate, yet it cannot be too time consuming, or the engine maintenance will not get done. There are always splices that need serving, sails that need stitching, and sheets that need whipping, and these chores must somehow be fitted into the daily routine of working the ship.

From time to time I have seen and remembered ideas that were being used to advantage aboard other people's yachts. Wherever possible, in this book, I have tried to identify these borrowed ideas and give proper credit to the men on whose yachts I saw them being used. In a few instances I have not been able to recall the sources, and in these cases I can only offer my apologies. For that matter, I have often worked out a design for an item on my own boat, only to run across another yacht on which the same feature had been in use for several years. I really doubt that there are many "original" ideas in yachts, if, by original, one means something which has never been thought of before.

The days of paid crews have long since vanished for most yachtsmen, and constantly increasing maintenance costs have swelled the ranks of those who "do it themselves." Quite apart from the economic pressure, though, I think most yachtsmen work on their own boats and rigging because they find this one of the most satisfying aspects of boat ownership. To have encountered a problem while cruising, to have thought about it and hit upon a solution, and to have seen one's own thought and labor eliminate the problem on one's own boat— this is one of the greatest satisfactions of sailing. Fortunately it is a source of satisfaction which is likely to last forever, since there seems to be an endless supply of problems.

L. R. B.

London, England, 1968

SHIPSHAPE AND BRISTOL FASHION

I
SAILS AND RIGGING

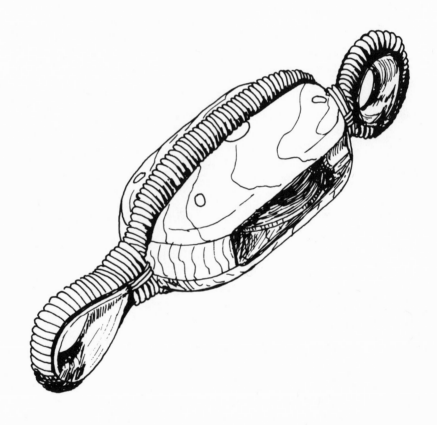

MAGAZINES FOR HEADSAILS

Nearly all the difficulties in handling headsails arise from the wind getting hold of the sail when it is not hanked to the stay or stowed in its bag. It is one thing to hank a sail on in a leisurely fashion at the dockside, and something quite different to manage this on a pitching, spray-swept foredeck with the wind howling past trying to pluck the sail out of your grasp. These magazines will go a long way toward eliminating many of those "embarrassing moments."

They consist of a length of wire rope about three feet long. I prefer to make them of flexible halyard wire, since they stow more easily. Put an eye in one end and serve the splice. You can eliminate the need for a shackle at this point, if you open the thimble and slip it through the eye of a snap hook before making the splice.

Cut some discs about two inches in diameter from some ¾ inch hardwood, as for instance locust or ash. Drill a hole in the center large enough to pass the wire rope. Sand the discs well and boil them in vegetable oil such as corn oil. Slide one of these onto the wire and jam it down against the eyesplice you have made. Just above it put a seizing on the wire to hold the disc in place. Now about two or two and a half feet from this disc, place another disc, held in place by a seizing on either side. You now have two discs fixed to the wire about two and a half feet apart. Six inches beyond the second disc, put in another eyesplice around a small thimble. Serve the splice and build up a ball-shaped mouse on the thimble. (See Figure 1.)

To use this magazine, snap the snap hook into the stemhead fitting or the eye at the bottom of the stay. Grasp the six-inch length beyond the second disc in your left hand (if you are right handed), and with the same hand hold onto the stay. The mouse on the end of the wire prevents it slipping out of your grasp, as you pull up on the end to keep it taut. The two discs hold the magazine wire away from the stay so that you can snap the jib hanks onto the magazine as soon as you remove them from the stay. In this way, there is never more than one hank at a time which is not attached either to the stay or to the magazine. Figure 2 shows a sail on the magazine, ready to be bagged.

When you bag the sail, stuff it in so the magazine goes in last. Then

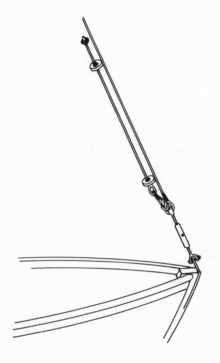

Fig. 1—Magazine in position on stay.

when you use it next time, it may be completely hanked on before the bulk of it is removed from the sail bag.

These magazines give the deck hand what is essentially another hand with which to work, and they can prevent a lot of embarrassing errors. For example, properly used they make it impossible to set a Genoa upside down. They will result in faster, smoother sail changes, and, not least in importance, they will almost guarantee that your headsails are kept out of the drink.

TRICING LINE FOR JIBS

It is not unusual to see a yachtsman drop his jib before sailing into a harbor, even though it is obvious that his boat handles better with two headsails. This is almost always attributed to the difficulty experienced in handling the jib or genoa when tacking. This tricing line will enable you to take your jib around the forestay with ease and without

Fig. 2—Headsail on magazine, ready to be bagged.

the help of an extra hand on the foredeck, even in light airs. It is very easy to make and rig, and it is easily taken off and stowed since it is attached by a simple snap shackle.

A small snap shackle snatch block will work well for this rig, or you may seize a snap shackle to the eye of a small single block. This is snapped to the jibstay above the jib hank which is *the first one above the miter line of the jib.* It will be carried aloft when the jib is set. The tricing line leads through this block down to another block at the stemhead, and back to the cockpit. (See Figure 3.)

The forward end of the tricing line ends in a toggle seized or spliced in the end of the line. I have seized mine in, since I like to use braided line for this, and I hate to splice the stuff.

In the jib, right on the miter line, and two-thirds of the way from the luff to the clew, sew a reinforcing patch, and work a grommet into the patch (see page 160 for details of made grommets). Into this grommet fix a becket consisting of an eyesplice in a piece of laid nylon or dacron line. Just above the splice, tie a Matthew Walker knot and lay up the strands for a few inches beyond the Matthew Walker. Pass the end through the grommet and draw the rope up until the Matthew Walker is tight up against the grommet. Then put on a stopper knot, such as a doubled wall and crown in the other side. Cut off the ends and melt them down with a candle.

The end of the tricing line is now toggled into this becket, and the rig is ready to use. When you come about and the jib luffs, haul on the tricing line. This will pull the jib forward far enough for the bulk

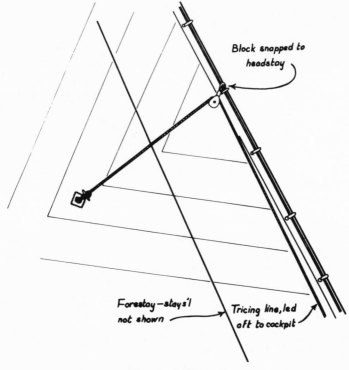

Block snapped to
headstay

Forestay—stays'l
not shown

Tricing line, led
aft to cockpit

Fig. 3—Tricing line.

of it to pass around the forestay, and the wind will do the rest when
you release the tricing line. It is simple and it adds a lot to shorthanded
sailing.

HANDMADE BLOCKS

Few things add as much to the appearance of a yacht as a matched
set of nicely varnished blocks, and there are few projects from which I
have derived so much satisfaction as from making a set myself. Actually, it is not a difficult job, and one added incentive might be the fact
that you can save a considerable sum of money in this way if you in-
tend to replace many of the blocks on your boat. I first became interested in block-making when I read H.G. Smith's excellent description

of it in his book *The Arts of the Sailor*,* and I am greatly in his debt
for the enjoyment this has given me. I differ with him, however, on one
basic point. Smith says that "mortised" blocks, that is, those cut from
a single piece of wood, are much easier to make than "made" blocks,
or those built up from several pieces. I have made quite a number of
both kinds, and I find that I consistently get better blocks more easily
by building them up. With all respect to Mr. Smith, therefore, I shall
describe the procedure which I find the easier—that for "made" blocks.

I suggest that you try making one single block to begin with. Much
time can be saved by carrying through all the steps on a number of
identical blocks at one time, but the experience gained from making
one trial block initially can help you avoid duplicating the same error
on all ten of a matched set.

Buy the sheave first, and get one with roller bearings. Its cost is still
insignificant compared with the cost of a good block and its ease of
operation is infinitely better than you can get with a plain bearing. At
the same time, buy a length of rod for the axle, and for this I prefer
stainless steel. Bronze will work as well at first, but it does wear more
rapidly in the way of the bearings.

With the sheave at hand, lay out an exact pattern for the block,
using Figure 4 as a guide. The following general rules will be of help:

1. The finished block should be as wide as the diameter of
   the sheave.
2. Its length from top to bottom should be about one and
   six-tenths sheave diameters.
3. Its thickness at the widest point should be a little more
   than two and one-half times the thickness of the sheave.
4. In the swallow below the sheave, there should be just
   enough clearance for the sheave to turn freely, but above
   it you should allow one and one-half rope diameters
   (sheave thicknesses) minimum clearance from the deepest part of the groove in the sheave.

Make full size patterns of the various pieces required (four in all)
on cardboard stiff enough to allow you to trace around them. Prick the

* Hervey Garrett Smith, *The Arts of the Sailor* (Princeton, N.J.: D. Van
Nostrand Company, Inc., 1953).

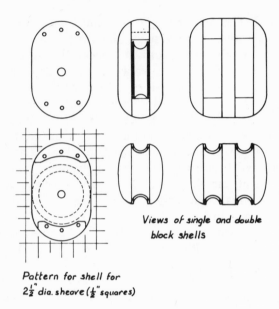

Views of single and double
block shells

Pattern for shell for
$2\frac{1}{2}''$ dia. sheave ($\frac{1}{4}''$ squares)

Fig. 4—Pattern for block shells.

centers of all holes which are to be drilled, so you may mark these on the wood.

Any hardwood will do for the block shells, with the possible exception of teak which contains too much oil to glue dependably. I have used nearly every type of hardwood, and I find that locust, ash, maple, elm, and walnut all make lovely blocks. I rather like to make the cheeks of locust or ash and the center spacers of a dark wood such as walnut. At any rate, have the wood planed to the thicknesses required —the center pieces will ordinarily be a little thicker than the cheeks. It is *very* important that you start with flat, parallel-sided pieces of wood. The center pieces should be cut from wood planed to be about $\frac{1}{16}$ inch thicker than the sheave you are using.

Start by tracing the outlines of two cheek pieces on the thinner wood. Mark the location of the center hole and of the six small pin holes. Saw these pieces a trifle oversize. Now trace another cheek outline on the thicker wood and saw it out. Check your drill press to make sure it is drilling at right angles to the work table.

Now lay the three pieces in a stack and adjust them until they are

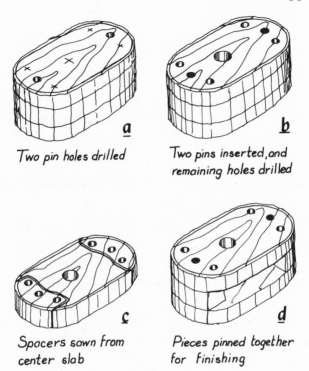

Two pin holes drilled

Two pins inserted, and
remaining holes drilled

Spacers sawn from
center slab

Pieces pinned together
for finishing

Fig. 5—Steps in construction of blocks.

as well lined up as you can get them. Clamp them together with a
C-clamp and drill two of the pin holes, as shown in Figure 5a. The
pins should be about ⅛ inch to ³/₁₆ inch in diameter, and the holes
should be a tight fit for them. Cut lengths of brass rod for the pins—
these should be about ¼ inch shorter than the finished thickness of
the blocks at the thickest point. Bevel the ends of the pins slightly
with a file, and drive two of them into the holes you have drilled.
These will now key the blocks together, and you can drill the other
pin holes and the axle hole through all three blocks at one time, thus
insuring that everything will fit accurately (Figure 5b).

Now separate the three pieces of wood, and take the thicker one
for the moment. Place your patterns for the spacer pieces over this
piece of wood, positioning them so that the pin holes you have
drilled line up with those marked on the patterns. Trace round the

patterns, as shown in Figure 5c. Saw along these lines and discard the center portion of this piece of wood.

You may now reassemble the slabs and pin them together with the brass pins (Figure 5d). It is well to mark the blocks, since no matter how carefully you drill the pin holes, they will always fit better in one certain way. With the pins holding the pieces in the proper relative positions, clamp the assembled block in the vise and finish it down to the marked outline, which should be visible on one of the cheek pieces. For this a coarse wood rasp works well.

Round off all the corners next with the rasp, leaving an even chamfer where all the corners were (Figure 6a). From this point on, you will find it difficult to hold the work in the vise. For the rest of the shaping, which I do on a disk sander with a very coarse, rather flexible disk, I always work by eye with the work in my hands. If you feel the need for it, a template cut from cardboard will help to keep the block symmetrical as you shape it to final form. Keep the work moving continually so you do not cut flat faces on it with the sanding disk.

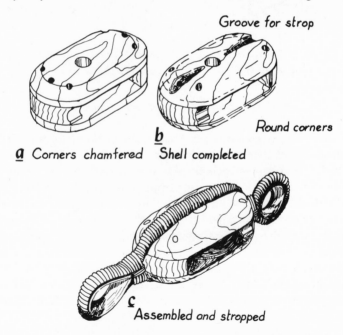

Groove for strop

Round corners

a Corners chamfered   **b** Shell completed

c Assembled and stropped

Fig. 6—Construction of blocks (cont.).

Change to a fine sanding disk for the finish, and then give the entire outer surface a final hand-sanding with some very fine paper such as 400 wet or dry. The outer surfaces are now finished. Separate the parts of the block and finish the inner surfaces of the spacers. I don't spend too much time on these, but I do check them to be sure there is ample clearance around the sheave, as well as to be certain that the sheave will slide into the swallow of the block when the wood pieces are assembled. Round the edges of the swallows where the rope enters and leaves the block, and it is ready to assemble (Figure 6b).

Mix some resorcinol or epoxy glue, and coat the mating surfaces of the pieces with it. Reassemble the pieces and clamp them tightly in a vise or clamp until the glue is set. Remove the excess glue, sand the glue lines lightly, and give the shell a coat of varnish thinned with an equal amount of turpentine.

When this has dried, cut a groove for the strop in the sides of the block with a rat-tail file. When I do not plan to use a becket, I like to run the groove all the way around the bottom of the block. However, if the block is to have a becket, do *not* run the groove around the bottom, but fade it out as you do for the upper end. Now give the finished shell seven or eight coats of varnish, sanding between each coat. While this is drying, you can make the axle and the strop.

Cut the axle to length from the rod you have bought for this purpose, and bevel the corners at the ends. When the block is assembled, the axle should be just flush with the face of the cheek on either side. Make a couple of washers from some brass shim stock to go on either side of the sheave. This will keep it from rubbing against the sides of the swallow. Check the edges of the groove in the sheave for nicks or cuts which might damage your rope, and remove these with a fine file and emery cloth. Pack the bearing with waterproof grease and insert the sheave and axle.

I have made strops in a host of different ways, and they all work. I have finally settled on a wire strop made by short-splicing the ends of a length of 7 x 7 wire, which I serve over with marline and seize on with the splice either at the bottom of the block or forming the eye in the thimble at the top. If you do not care to try the wire splicing, you can have your rigger make the strops for you, or you can make them of prestretched dacron sold for halyards.

If you use the dacron, unlay a length of the rope and lay up one strand into a grommet, tucking the ends once before paring down the strand to half the diameter, and tucking this remainder twice. The grommet should be large enough so that you can just squeeze it together between the block and thimble before it is served. Serve it over with some $\frac{1}{16}$ inch nylon braid or fishline. An excellent explanation of grommet-making can be found in Ashley's *Book of Knots* * or H. G. Smith's *The Arts and Crafts of the Sailor.*

If you have a stainless strop, you may serve it or not as you choose, since it needs no protection from the weather. I often serve only that portion of the strop which will come in contact with the shell of the block, leaving bare the portion which will lie in the thimble at the top and the area which will receive the seizing.

For the seizing I prefer seizing wire (dead soft) for a wire strop, or $\frac{3}{32}$ inch nylon braid for a rope strop. There is enough elasticity in the nylon so that with each turn you accumulate tension in the seizing. To help distribute this, grease the nylon with vaseline before beginning the seizing. Make one end fast to the strop and begin taking the first layer of seizing turns. Haul each turn as tight as you can get it. If you suceed in pulling the strop completely closed, continue your seizing turns to the point where the strop begins to separate in spite of your efforts.

Now clamp the block, wrapped in cloth to protect the varnish, in your vise, and put on a layer of riding turns, heaving each of these as tight as you can get it. Finish with three or four frapping turns and a couple of single hitches (Figure 6c).

After you have recovered from this, remove the block from the vise and admire it. There may be one or two things about it that you will want to change in your subsequent blocks, but even so it will be a lovely thing to look at and lovelier still to use. It will be quiet, almost frictionless, and unique.

In your later efforts, you will want to cut all your pieces at one time, carry through all the drilling at one go, and otherwise take advantage of the time-saving opportunities inherent in making several identical blocks. You can make a wide variety of shapes and sizes, with and without beckets, etc.

If you have or can get access to a lathe, you may wish to make some sheaves. Your chandler has, or can get for you, roller bearing bushes for sheaves as shown in Figure 7. You can turn your own sheaves, from

* Clifford W. Ashley, *Ashley Book of Knots* (Garden City, N.Y.: Doubleday & Company, Inc., 1944).

Roller bearing insert   Hardwood sheave with
roller insert

Fig. 7—Details of sheave construction.

live oak or locust, with a recess in the center into which the roller bush can be mounted. These wooden sheaves are very light in weight, completely noiseless, and, if they are soaked in vegetable cooking oil for two or three weeks, they require no care at all. They do have the added advantage of being available in any diameter in which you wish to make them, and this can be a real advantage for certain special applications for which the commercially available sizes will not do.

KEEPERS FOR RUNNING BACKSTAYS

Many cruising sailboats still carry running backstays, and not without some justification. In a cutter rig—my hands-down choice for a single sticker—they constitute the most effective means of keeping a tight luff on the staysail without introducing the excessive compression stresses caused by jumper struts and stays. Eliminating jumper struts gets rid of a major cause of fouled halyards, and this is a big gain in itself.

The most common objection to running backstays is that they complicate coming about and jibing. I have found that this just isn't so, once one gets used to them, and one gets used to them very quickly. My biggest objection, when I first cruised a boat with runners, was the need to leave the cockpit and go forward to tie down the lee runner when it was slacked off. I don't like to see them slatting about chafing the mainsail.

I devised the keepers illustrated in Figure 8, and they have been a real joy to use, enabling me to handle the runners entirely from the cockpit. They are made of light nylon line, ending in a shackle which is a loose sliding fit on the backstay. The nylon line is led through

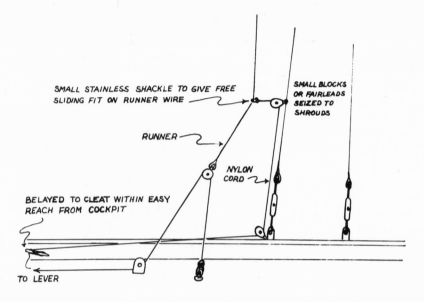

Fig. 8—"Keepers" for running backstays.

blocks or bullseyes in the shrouds, and back to cleats on the toerail alongside the cockpit.

Hauling in on this keeper pulls the runner well forward to the shrouds and away from the sail, and at the same time takes the slack out of the runner to prevent its flogging around. The position of the fairleads for the nylon should be adjusted by trial and error so that the runner is pulled forward clear of the sail where the sail's greatest belly develops while running off the wind.

With these keepers installed, shorthanded sailing with running backstays is little if any more complicated than with a standing backstay only, and one does have the extra bit of staying for the mast which can be very cheering in really bad weather.

BOOM PREVENTER

The more nearly all the yacht's gear can be carried so that it is instantly ready for use, the more likely it is to *be* used when it should be. A boom preventer is a must when running before the wind, especially with a light breeze and a following sea. All too often, however, a preventer is not rigged until its desirability is made evident by an accidental jibe. I suspect that this is usually because rigging a preventer from scratch is a time consuming job which often means calling another hand on deck. Even when set up, the ordinary preventer complicates matters when jibing becomes necessary, since it must be unrove forward, taken around the mast and shrouds, and rerove on the other side.

If a wire rope is permanently secured to the boom end by the fitting to which the sheets and topping lift attach, it is always in place and ready for instant use. The forward end of this wire should terminate in a snap shackle, and should be just long enough to reach a pad eye located on the after side of the mast just below the gooseneck. On larger boats, it is helpful to attach a pelican hook to the pad eye. If this is adjusted properly, it will put just enough strain on the wire to keep it taut and out of the way below the boom (Figure 9).

A nylon line ending in a hard eye is carried on the deck, rove

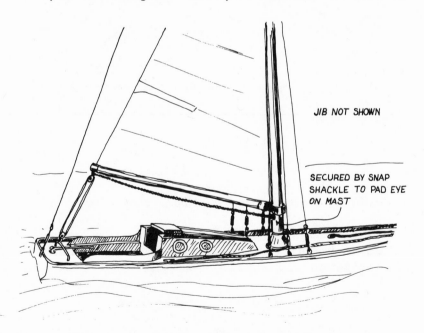

JIB NOT SHOWN

SECURED BY SNAP SHACKLE TO PAD EYE ON MAST

Fig. 9—Boom preventer stowed when not in use.

through a swivel block attached to the stemhead fitting. I like nylon because it has a little elasticity, and I like it long enough to make it possible to adjust the preventer from the cockpit. To rig the preventer for use, it is only necessary to release the wire from the eye on the mast and snap it to the hard eye in the nylon outside the shrouds. To jibe, one needs only to unsnap the shackle, take the preventer to the other side, and snap it together again outside the shrouds. The long nylon line remains rove all the while (Figure 10).

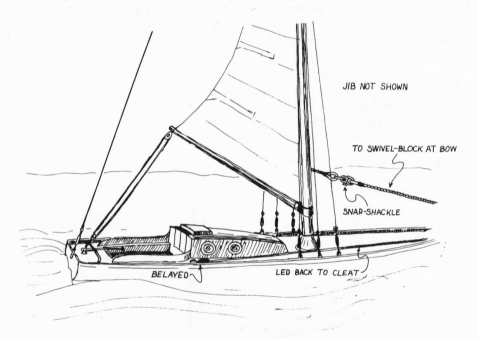

Fig. 10—Boom preventer set up on starboard tack.

Carried as shown, this preventer works equally well on a roller boom, and a reef may be rolled in without disturbing the wire stowed beneath the boom.

BELAYING HOOKS FOR HALYARDS

I have long been an ardent advocate of downhaul tackles for the tacks of headsails, and for mains and mizzens as well whenever a sliding gooseneck is available. I see no point in exerting myself to set up a sail's luff tightly with the weight of the sail working against me. It makes much more sense to hoist the sail, belay the halyard, and then to tighten the luff by hauling the tack down with the help of the weight of the sail.

I made up my current headsail halyards with this in mind. I first made two rings from ¼ inch stainless steel rod, each about two inches in diameter. I opened a wire thimble, slipped it onto the ring, and then bent it back to shape. The wire halyard was spliced in place around this thimble, and the splice was served. I next worked a rope thimble over the ring in the same manner and spliced the $9/16$ inch diameter dacron into this.

Then I turned out two wooden handles shaped as shown in Figure 11. These were made from ash and well varnished. I slipped one of these over the wire and slid it down to where it jammed against the splice in the ring. A mouse of seizing wire built up on the halyard

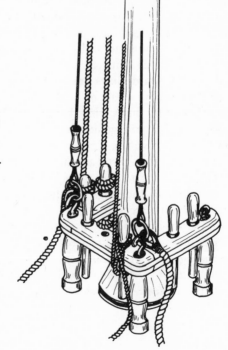

Fig. 11—Belaying hooks for halyards.

above the handle holds it firmly in place, and a Turkshead can be worked over the seizing wire. I now did some very careful measuring for the length of the halyard, passed it through the halyard block, and spliced a swivel snap shackle in the other end. The halyard must be just long enough to place the headsail at the desired height when the ring is hooked in place as shown in Figure 11. The splices were served and the end of the dacron line was whipped.

These halyard hooks are a real joy to use. The sail is simply hauled up and the ring is hooked in place. This automatically positions the sail correctly and takes all the strain off the fiber part of the halyard. The luff is then tightened by means of the tack downhaul. The wooden handles enable one to hook the rings in place, even when there is quite a wind blowing into the sail. Without them it is difficult to get a grip on the wire.

This tackle should be planned to position properly your highest-setting headsail. Pendants are then made for the other sails to set them where you want them. Pendants will also be necessary for the tacks of some of the sails. Make these overly long at first, bending a temporary eye in them until the correct length is established by actual trial, after which a permanent hard eye may be spliced in. This is a good time, too, to mark the head and tack clearly on your sails with laundry ink. Before I did this, someone was always setting my Genoa upside down.

If your halyard cleats are on the mast, this system can be used by mounting thumb cleats or hooks above the halyard cleats and hooking the rings onto these. Had I had a sliding gooseneck, I should have made a similar arrangement for the main halyard, although one would still have to have the cleat to use when the sail was reefed. As it is, I had to settle for a two-part main halyard instead.

Dropping the sails is simply a matter of letting go the tack downhauls, slipping the rings off the hooks, and letting the sail drop. A friend of mine recently suggested that I could end the dacron lines in snaps so they could be removed and stowed once the sail was set. This would make a nice clean deck arrangement for a racing craft, but for a cruising boat, often sailed by guests who might not know where the dacron line was stowed, I prefer to have the halyard permanently attached and ready for instant use.

TOGGLE AND BECKET FOR
HEADSAIL SHEET FASTENING

Snap shackles, especially in the larger sizes, are expensive items. They require frequent oiling if they are to work well, and they are not infallible by any means. I have had two of them, carrying the stamp of a leading manufacturer and of more than adequate size, break within a week of my having bought them—in both cases due to an obvious internal defect in the metal. They are hard and heavy, and their lethal potentialities on the clew of a flogging headsail are well appreciated by experienced yachtsmen.

In spite of these drawbacks, I had accepted the snap shackle as an indispensable item for headsail sheets until I saw these toggle and becket fastenings made up by Joe and Mary Cronk for their lovely little ketch, *Jane Louise*. They are easy to make, light in weight, very positive in their function, and quick and easy to release. They are also fun to make and never fail to elicit favorable comments from visitors aboard.

The basic secret of this fitting consists of selecting sheets of such a diameter that, when they are doubled, the bight can just be passed through the clew cringle. If the line is too large, the sheets will be difficult to attach, and if it is too small, they will tend to jam and be difficult to release. If your present sheets are good and not of the correct size to fit your clew cringles, splice a pendant into the clew of your headsails and end it in a hard eye of the proper size made around a sail thimble. This pendant need be only long enough for the splices.

To make the fastening, middle the sheet and side-splice it to a short length of line of the same diameter as the sheet itself (Figure 12a). Now put a racking seizing around the two parts of the sheet leaving a soft eye some four or five inches long beyond the seizing. Serve over the seizing and the side splice as shown in Figure 12b.

Four or five inches beyond the end of the soft eye, tie a Matthew Walker knot in the short length of line. Lay up the line for four or five inches beyond the Matthew Walker, whip it at this point, and cut it off.

To use this arrangement, squeeze the soft eye in your hand until

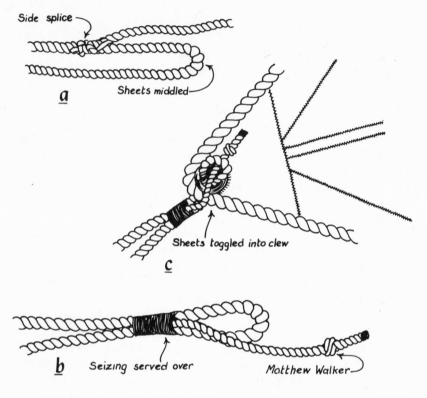

Fig. 12—Toggle and becket for headsail sheet fastening.

you can pass it through the cringle. Open the eye beyond the cringle, and pass the short line through it, pulling the Matthew Walker through the eye. Pull hard enough on the sheets to remove the slack in the eye. The sheets are now securely attached to the sail, since the eye plus the line forming the toggle add up to more bulk than will pass through the cringle (Figure 12c). The fastening can easily be released, however, by pulling on the tail beyond the Matthew Walker to gain a little slack, and then slipping the toggle out of the becket.

This same fitting should work equally well for halyards, and can be used with braided sheets as well as with laid sheets. Since there is no strain at all on the side splice shown in the drawing, a seizing will serve just as well. The easiest way to secure the toggle, when using braided stuff, is to sew it to one side of the bight of the sheets with sail twine, and then proceed to seize and serve the eye. Of course, with braided line you cannot use the Matthew Walker for the stopper knot, but a figure-of-eight will do just as well.

Toggles and beckets, either of this type or with the conventional wooden toggle, can be used to advantage in many places on a cruising boat. Tack pendants and downhauls, boom preventers, halyards, topping lifts—almost any application where snap shackles are ordinarily used. They are quiet, reliable, require little or no maintenance other than an occasional examination for chafe, and you won't be maimed if you get hit by them.

MASTHEAD SHEAVES

Removing your mast as a part of the winter lay-up procedure has a lot to be said for it. It gives you a chance to do a proper job of refinishing, as well as an opportunity to see to the rigging details that are so difficult to do aloft. Whether or not you remove the stick, don't forget to check the condition of the masthead sheaves, especially if your boat is an old one.

The first time I removed the main halyard sheave from *Viking "S,"* I realized why it had taken so much effort to tighten the luff of the main. The sheave was years old, had originally been galvanized, was rusted badly, and the bearing hole was in foul shape. The axle bolt was worn nearly halfway through on the upper surface. There was obviously no answer but a new sheave, and since I planned to re-rig with stainless wire, getting rid of a galvanized sheave was in the order of business anyway.

The first change I envisioned was a significant increase in diameter, since the halyard had been cutting into the wood of the mast where it left the swallow. I designed a new sheave large enough to keep the leads well clear of the mast on both sides, and this turned out to be larger than I expected. As you will see in Figure 13a, it is not enough that the *flanges* of the sheave project beyond the swallow cheeks— the *deepest part of the groove* must lie well outside the mast.

I turned out an oversized pattern from white pine, cut out the wood between the spokes to lighten the casting, and had this cast in bronze. It was still a heavy casting, but by the time I had machined it the weight was reduced to less than two pounds including the bear-

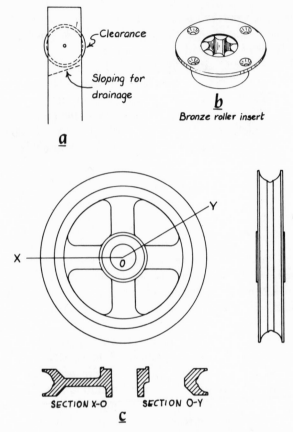

Fig. 13—Details of masthead sheave.

ing insert. I turned a recess in the hub to take a bronze roller-bearing insert, and mounted this with four machine screws. Notice in Figure 13c that the width at the hub is very slightly larger than the width at the flanges, to avoid any chafe between the flanges and the inside of the swallow.

I next made a box-shaped liner for the swallow from thin stainless steel, allowing just enough clearance for the sheave to turn easily. This can be a great safety factor, since it completely prevents the wire from wearing a space into which it can jam between the sheave and the cheek of the swallow. If you have never had a wire halyard jump off a sheave and jam in this fashion, consider yourself lucky and take my word for the fact that it can create quite a nasty problem in a strong wind with a sail halfway down. The bottom of the swallow should slope as in Figure 13a so that rain water will not collect to cause rot.

I used a stainless steel pin for the axle or shaft, forming a head on one end and threading the other for a hexagonal nut. Since this was larger in diameter than the original shaft, I had only to ream out the holes in the masthead fitting to accommodate it. The bearing was well packed with grease and the sheave mounted. After the nut was run down to the desired tightness, I cut off the excess shafting and upset the end lightly to keep the nut from running off.

The difference between this and the old sheave is difficult to describe. The sail runs up and down without a hint of resistance. The ruggedness of the bronze rollers, which I was inclined to doubt at first, has been amply demonstrated. When I replaced the engine last year, I hoisted the old engine out on the main halyard and set the new one in place the same way. This was a net load of over eight hundred pounds for the new engine, and the bearings show no sign of damage or distortion. This gives me a welcome feeling of security when I go aloft on the main halyard.

You will notice in Figure 13c, that I have shown a double groove for rope and wire. I use a two part halyard on the main, and this design is necessary. If your rig requires that both fiber and wire rope run through the sheave, a double groove should definitely be used. The groove for the wire should be of a little larger radius than the wire and slightly less than half a diameter in depth. Its edges should be carefully finished and polished to avoid any possible damage to the fiber rope.

For the benefits it will offer, this project is not a particularly involved one. It is one which will give you real satisfaction and pride when it is done, and which should last for almost the life of the yacht. An annual greasing will assure long life from the bearings, and they can be replaced if they ever do wear out. It might be a good idea to buy an extra bearing insert of the same size and stow it with your spares, since companies do go out of business or change models from time to time.

BOOM GUYS

If your yacht has a sturdy gallows for the main boom, the main sheets will serve as adequate guys when the boom is stowed. If not, such guys are very much worth making up. The frequently seen scissors type crutch provides an ample amount of lateral bracing for the boom, but this type of crutch is a real menace and I would not have one aboard a cruising boat. On the other hand, the simple vertical type of crutch, which is quite safe and generally satisfactory if it is heavily enough built, gives very little lateral bracing.

In harbor, of course, one encounters no great amount of rolling, so this concern over lateral support is not relevant, and the main sheet carries the load at sea, when the mainsail is set and pulling. The problem arises during bad weather at sea when the mainsail has been handed and furled and the trysail is set. The rolling motion of the boat makes the main boom tend to swing from side to side, and the almost vertical pull of the main sheet does little if anything to prevent this. I have a very heavy crutch made from steel pipe which sets in a sturdy socket bolted to a bulkhead. After one especially nasty bit of weather, during which we were under trysail and storm jib for two days and bare poles and a sea anchor for two more, I found the steel crutch had been badly bent just above the socket.

I made up two ten-foot guys from ½ inch diameter dacron, whipping one end of each and putting an eyesplice in the other end. They have solved the problem completely. As soon as the mainsail is down and furled, and the boom is lowered into the crutch, the two guys are attached to the boom just abaft the crutch. This is easily done by sticking the whipped end through the eye to form a noose. A bit of canvas around the boom and sail eliminates chafe at this point. The ends of the guys are brought downward and outward to the main sheet cleats on the deck, and set up as tightly as possible.

Since I made these, we have been using them routinely in harbor, as well. They are quick to set up, and they spare the main sheet the needless wear from the slight movement through the sheet blocks if the yacht is rolling at all.

LANOLIN FOR TURNBUCKLES AND SHACKLE PINS

I think I must have tried almost every type of grease available in an attempt to prevent rust and malfunction of turnbuckles and shackle pins, and nothing seemed to do much good until I tried lanolin. This idea comes from Eric Hiscock, who has already mentioned it in his own writings, but it works so unbelievably well that it deserves repeating.

Get anhydrous lanolin from your druggist. A pound jar is quite inexpensive and will last through several seasons. At the end of each season, I go through my shackle bucket and clean up all the shackle pins with a steel brush. Then I dip the threaded end of each in lanolin, and screw the pins back in the shackles. I know, now, when I grab a shackle from the bucket that I'll be able to unscrew the pin with my fingers.

Last winter I put out a third anchor, as we were lying in a very unprotected harbor and the violence of the wind sometimes had to be felt to be believed. I used three lengths of steel wire rope for the rode, shackling these together with lanolin-treated shackles. When I took this anchor up after six months, I was able to open all of the shackles with my fingers after I had removed the safety wires.

After tuning my rigging at the beginning of the season, I pack each turnbuckle with lanolin. Then a two-inch wide strip of heavy plastic sheeting is wrapped, like a bandage, around the turnbuckle from bottom to top. Wrapped in this direction, it acts like shingles on a roof and seems to admit very little water. It is held at the upper end by a doubled constrictor knot. The plastic sheeting is elastic enough to mould itself tightly to the irregular shape of the turnbuckle if it is stretched as it is applied. When there is any need for adjusting the turnbuckles, the plastic can be removed very quickly and the threads are always free and easy to move.

I know that the ideal answer to these problems of rust and corrosion is supposed to be stainless steel, and I'd have it throughout, including the anchor chain if I could get it and were able to afford it. As it is, I still have to make do with turnbuckles and shackles which were *originally* galvanized, but with lanolin for a grease I have no more problems with their freezing up.

A DOUBLE-ENDED HALYARD FOR
THE MIZZEN STAYSAIL

The mizzen staysail is a wonderful reaching sail, and the ability to carry it more than justifies the ketch or yawl rig for a cruising boat. Many such boats, however, carry standing main backstays which are led to the mizzen mast, often at the point where the mizzen shrouds or running backstays are attached. This usually makes for complications when tacking or jibing with the mizzen staysail, since the halyard must be unshackled from the head of the sail, thrown up and over the backstay, and re-shackled to the sail before the sail can be set on the other side. Throwing the halyard over the backstay sounds easy, but in any kind of wind the halyard often fouls in the shrouds and creates an annoying delay and confusion.

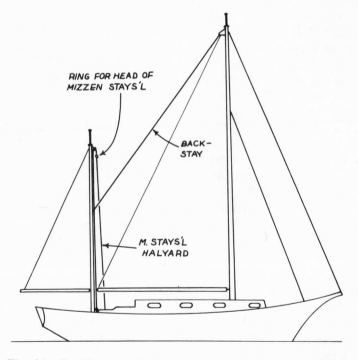

RING FOR HEAD OF
MIZZEN STAYS'L

BACK-
STAY

M. STAYS'L
HALYARD

Fig. 14—Double-ended halyard for mizzen staysail (sideview).

This double-ended halyard (Figure 14) was shown to me by Joe Barnett, who made it up for *Rama Dorada* when he skippered her across the Atlantic in 1966. It seems to solve the problem, since it can be kept under control at all times. It consists of a length of flexible wire rope, on each end of which an eye is spliced into a stainless steel ring about two inches in diameter. Into each of these rings the rope hauling parts of the halyard are spliced. These dacron tails should be a little longer than the height of the halyard block above the deck. (See Figure 15.)

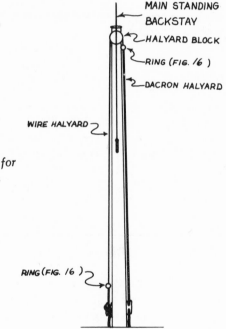

MAIN STANDING BACKSTAY

HALYARD BLOCK

RING (FIG. *16*)

DACRON HALYARD

WIRE HALYARD

RING (FIG. *16*)

Fig. 15—Double-ended halyard for mizzen staysail (looking aft).

A snap shackle is seized into the head of the mizzen staysail, and this is snapped into the ring on the leeward end of the halyard (Figure 16). The sail is set flying by hauling on the other end. When the sail is set, very little of the dacron line is in use, nearly all the strain being on the wire portion.

To jibe, the sail is dropped and the snap shackle is removed from the ring in the halyard. The other end of the halyard is pulled down within reach, and the sail is snapped to it, while the tack is moved

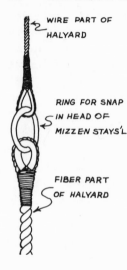

WIRE PART OF
HALYARD

RING FOR SNAP
IN HEAD OF
MIZZEN STAYS'L

FIBER PART
OF HALYARD

Fig. 16—Detail of ring in mizzen staysail halyard.

to the other end of the mast. The sail can now be hoisted on the other side of the backstay and the halyard belayed.

In actual practice, especially on a cruising yacht, the entire halyard could be made from prestretched halyard dacron. This is not a sail for use close-hauled, and the very little stretch found in this material should not adversely affect the sail's performance when off the wind.

SHOCK-CORD KEEPER FOR TOPPING LIFTS

If a topping lift is trimmed tightly enough to prevent its flogging about when the boom is well out, it will be too tight when the sail has to be sheeted in flat. This often makes for considerable extra work in going forward to trim the topping lift each time the sail's trim is changed significantly, since a flogging topping lift can cause a surprising amount of chafe on the leach during a long passage.

This problem has been very neatly solved by Stanley Woodward Jr. on his lovely old yawl, *Belisarius*. His solution is to seize a long piece of shock-cord to the topping lift about half way to the masthead. This is led through a couple of bullseyes seized to the backstay, and then down to a cleat at deck level (Figure 17). The whole secret lies in having the upper bullseye considerably below the point where the shock-cord is seized to the topping lift. This allows the boom to move some

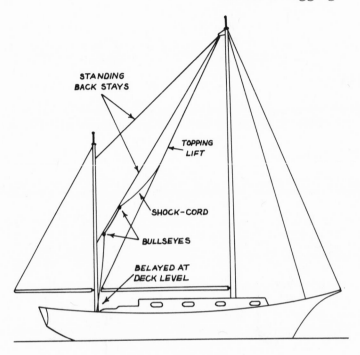

STANDING
BACK STAYS

TOPPING
LIFT

SHOCK-CORD

BULLSEYES

BELAYED AT
DECK LEVEL

Fig. 17—Shock-cord "keeper" for topping lift.

distance from side to side without markedly altering the tension on the shock-cord.

This "keeper" has to be adjusted, of course, if extreme changes are made in the trim of the sail, but the shock-cord is elastic enough to take care of all minor changes in trim. Even when the trim has to be altered, this can be done from the cockpit, and the topping lift itself can be left set up for sailing close hauled, and consequently never has to be changed.

SAIL TRACK OILERS

A mainsail that does not drop when the halyard is released is more than annoying—it is a menace. Its reluctance is almost always due to lack of lubrication of the sail track, a chore often neglected if one must go aloft each time in order to do it.

I had seen and copied several different devices for oiling my track, and had employed all of them with rather indifferent success. It wasn't until I worked out this design for some friends of mine that I really solved the problem. I now have made one for myself and highly recommend it to others.

I shall describe first the construction of the simpler type, shown in Figure 18b, for internal or English style track.

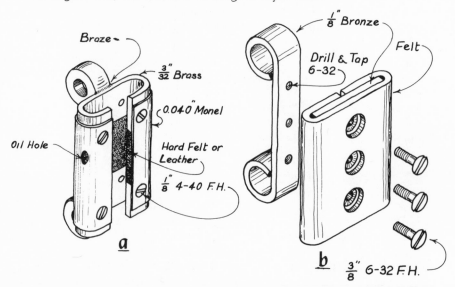

Fig. 18—Sail track oilers.

Start with some brass or bronze sheet rock, and some felt such as a piece from an old hat. Two thicknesses of the felt plus one of the brass should be just thick enough to fill the slot in your track, so measure the track first and select the material accordingly. The height of the brass or bronze rectangle should be about two and one-half inches. Its width should be the internal width of your track less three thicknesses of the felt. Lay it out accordingly and cut and file it to size, rounding the edges and corners slightly.

Bend the back piece from a section of brass or bronze strip just a little narrower than the gap in your sail track. Form the rings on the ends and solder the joints if there is any question of their opening under strain. Now clamp the two pieces of brass together and drill the three screw holes with a tap size drill. Tap the holes in the back piece, which has the rings at the ends. Drill out the holes in the rectangle to clear the screws and countersink for the screw heads.

Cut the felt the same width as the brass and long enough to wrap around and meet in the back. In the center line, mark the position of the screw holes and cut holes in the felt large enough to pass the screw heads. A large punch is the easy answer here, although a small penknife blade will do the trick. Cut out some V-shaped notches where the ends of the felt would interfere with the screws between the two brass pieces.

Assemble the oiler, setting up the machine screws tightly. Keep the felt as tight as possible while you do this.

Attach the oiler with a nylon lanyard so that it is positioned just below the top slide on the sail. From the lower ring on the oiler, run a second lanyard down to the second sail slide to pull the oiler down when the sail is lowered. There should be just enough slack in the nylon to allow the luff to be stretched tight.

Saturate the felt with light oil, such as sewing-machine oil, and blot off the excess. Now each time you raise or lower the sail, the track will be cleaned and oiled automatically.

To make the second type of oiler, shown in Figure 18a, for American style track, obtain a bar of iron about seven or eight inches long with a cross section a little larger than the horizontal portion of the "T" section of your sail track. You will use this as a mandrel, so round the corners lightly and smooth any gross nicks or irregularities for a distance of three or four inches from one end. Clamp the other end firmly in a bench vise. Cut a template from thin sheet iron—an empty can will do—to serve as a pattern for forming the brass channel. It should be about three inches high and wide enough to wrap around the mandrel leaving a large enough gap to clear the center section of the track. Trace this shape on some $\frac{3}{32}$ inch brass stock, and cut it out with a saw. Be sure the brass is soft enough to form cold without cracking. The rings could be formed out of tabs left at the upper and lower centers of this piece, but I found it simpler to make them separately and hard solder them to the channel when it was finished.

Bend the brass plate around the mandrel, shaping it with a mallet as you go. When you think you have it finished, remove it and try it on your sail track. It should be a free-sliding fit with no binding in any position. Round the corners and edges with a file.

Now cut a rectangle from a thinner piece of stock—I happened to have some Monel at hand, so I used that. It should be $\frac{3}{4}$ inch shorter than the brass channel and wide enough to wrap around as shown in the illustration. Slip the brass back on the mandrel and form this piece of Monel around the outside of it. Round the edges and corners and finish them flush with the brass at the gap in the channel.

Center punch and drill the brass and Monel together for the flat head machine screws used to join these pieces. Make four holes in the front surface and four in the back, using a tap size drill for the screws you plan to use—⅛ inch No. 4-40 flat heads are about right. Separate the two pieces and tap the holes in the brass channel. Drill out the holes in the Monel with a clear size drill and countersink them. It will be helpful in doing this to fit the formed Monel over a wooden mandrel while it is being drilled and countersunk.

Make up the brass rings and solder one to each end of the brass channel, keeping clear of the space the Monel will occupy at either end. It will help to draw a line across, ⅜ inch from each end of the brass, and keep the ring and solder clear of this.

Now make two saw cuts across the brass channel, removing the center section entirely. You can discard this. Obtain some felt about ⅛ inch thick—rather hard felt is best, and can usually be had from your cobbler. Assemble the brass pieces and the Monel with the machine screws and accurately measure the width of the gap where you sawed out the section of brass—cut the felt into a strip exactly this wide or perhaps just a hair wider. It can be cut with shears, although I find that a razor blade leaves a better edge. Drill the oil hole as shown in the sketch.

Wrap the felt strip around the iron mandrel, and assemble the oiler around it, letting the felt take the place of the brass you have cut out. Trim the ends of the felt strip flush at the gap in the channel —again, a razor blade works well. The felt should be stiff enough to hold itself securely in place. Saturate it well with oil; a very light oil such as sewing-machine oil is best. Attach the oiler with a nylon lanyard as described before, and the oiler is ready for use.

These oilers serve two valuable functions. They oil the track, and they also scrub off the film of oil and dust which otherwise eventually builds up into a gummy deposit on the track. Every couple of days, while cruising, make sure the felt is oily to the touch, and the rest of the work is done automatically when you raise and lower the sail. Avoid a great excess of oil—the felt needs only enough to make it feel oily to your finger.

II
SPARS AND BOWSPRITS

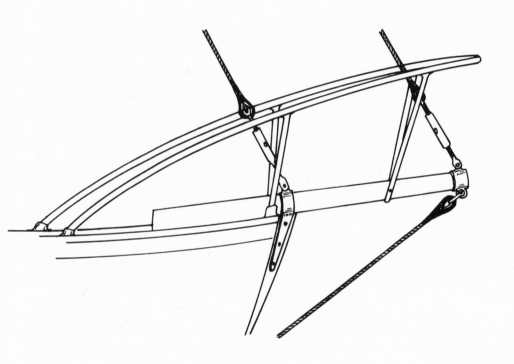

A MODIFIED SPINNAKER POLE

We have given up the use of a spinnaker for cruising. It requires too much coordinated effort to handle, and I have come to regard it as a dangerous sail. Just last season, for example, a copy of Eric Tabarly's single hander, *Pen Duick II*, was coming down along the Portuguese coast. The owner had been on the foredeck trying to maneuver a spinnaker pole, when the sail filled with a sudden gust of wind and flipped him overboard. He was never found.

We still carry a spinnaker pole, however, and use it very frequently. By winging out the staysail with it on one side and setting the working or Genoa jib on the other, we have a very practical pair of running sails. They give us ample speed with a reasonable wind, and are wonderful before the wind at night since they eliminate the constant worry about an accidental jibe.

The spinnaker pole illustrated in Figure 19 is very easy to use, and is much safer than the conventional one. It works with a variety of sails, and can also be put to good use as a hoisting boom. You can make this pole from scratch, or modify your present one if it is large enough. The finished pole should be long enough to pole out your largest headsail, and it should be thick enough to carry this added length. Work out these dimensions carefully before you begin to work.

The inboard end of the pole carries a standard piston-type fitting, and this attaches to a heavy pad eye set in a horizontal position on the forward side of the mast. Clear of this end fitting, cut a swallow in the pole to admit a roller-bearing sheave for the outhaul line. This line need be no more than ½ inch in diameter, even for a fairly large yacht; anything much smaller is difficult to get a grip on. If you are lucky, you may be able to use the tangs of the spinnaker pole fitting to support the axle for the sheave, enlarging the end rivet holes to pass the axle bolt.

At the outboard end, cut a slot as shown in Figure 19, and then build up the upper side of the pole with two wooden blocks to increase the height at the outer end. This increase should be a little more than the diameter of the outhaul line. Round over the corners of these blocks and shape the end of the pole as shown.

Have the fitting made from stainless steel sheet, about .060 inch

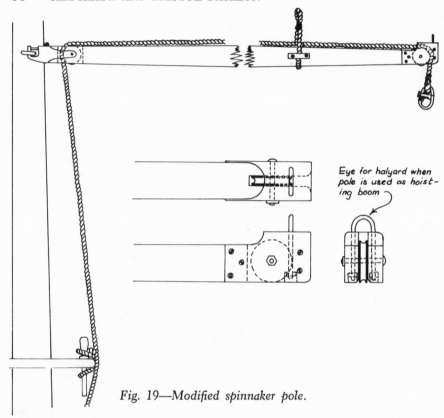

Eye for halyard when pole is used as hoisting boom

Fig. 19—Modified spinnaker pole.

thick. The holes for the screws should be countersunk and should be staggered so that the screws from opposite sides do not run into each other. The lifting eye can be bent from ¼ inch stainless rod, and welded to the fitting or supported by threading the ends and using nuts and washers. The "hooded" shape of the fitting, closing the top of the swallow as it does, prevents the outhaul line from jumping off the sheave when the pole is in use.

The strop and becket shown in Figure 19 are for the topping lift, which attaches by means of a toggle. The stowing chock is simply a block with a half round groove on its forward face to accommodate the pole. It is set on the forward side of the mast at the proper height to support the upper end of the pole when it is stowed vertically, and the topping lift is led through a block slung just below this chock.

To use this pole to wing out a headsail, first sheet in the sail until the clew can be reached from the deck. Lower the pole from its chock and let it rest on the taut headsail sheet. Snap the end of the outhaul line into the clew of the sail. Now go back to the mast where there is something to hold on to, have your crew slack off the headsail sheet, and haul the clew out by the outhaul to the exact point where you want it. Belay the outhaul to the pin rail and the job is done. To get rid of the pole, simply slack off the outhaul, unsnap the line from the clew of the sail, and raise the pole to its stowing position. None of your work need be done while you are balancing on tiptoe, and you always have a free hand with which to hold on.

If a couple of additional pad eyes are made for the inboard end of the pole and mounted on the port and starboard faces of the mast, the pole may be used to real advantage for lifting heavy articles aboard or ashore. It can be swung aft over the cockpit, and the main halyard or topping lift used for the lifting tackle. I have found this very useful in removing pigs of inside ballast and swinging them ashore, the ballast being hoisted through the open skylight in a canvas bucket and swung directly ashore on the pole. Alongside a quay, it makes for easy loading of heavy stores.

It also makes a fine boat boom to which your dinghy can be made fast. If you guy the pole fore and aft and let it extend straight out from the yacht's side, it will hold the dinghy clear and still allow you to pull it alongside if the outhaul is slacked off. This keeps the dinghy ready to use, but protects the topsides of the yacht without the use of fenders.

END-FITTING FOR ROLLER BOOM

We continue to do a lot of things in the same old way simply because no one ever stops to ask if there might not be a better approach. When I re-rigged V*iking* "S," I cut a couple of feet off the end of her boom and made a new end fitting as shown in Figure 20. After I had mounted it, I was sitting on deck one afternoon when a yacht designer came along and struck up a conversation. He remarked on the nice fitting, and then said, "You have it on upside down, though. I'm sure the designer intended the two arms of the 'Y' to point upwards."

I assured him that the designer had not intended this at all, and finally overcame his persistence by informing him that I was the designer,

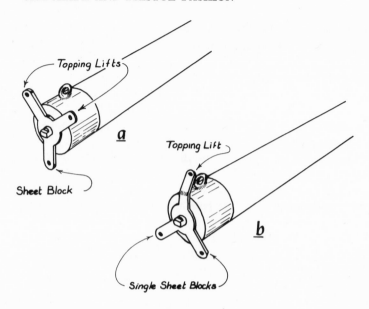

Fig. 20—End fitting for a roller reefing boom.

and that in this particular instance, at least, we did not have to specu-
late about the designer's intentions.

Many end fittings of this general design are seen on yachts with
roller-reefing booms, and very frequently the two arms *do* point upwards, often being joined by a jumper link from which the topping lift
is slung, while a double or treble block hangs from the single arm
below for the sheets. This, of course, made sense in the old days of
gaff riggers, since they carried two topping lifts. Used in this fashion
on a Bermudian rigged yacht, the fitting not only looks ridiculous—it
fails to function as well as it should.

Whenever the sheet is led through quarter blocks on deck, it should
never be rove through a multiple block at the boom end. If you doubt
this, take a close look at such a rig—there are plenty of examples in
any yacht harbor. You will see that the sheet has worn deep grooves in
the cheeks of the blocks, and of course it will have chafed itself merci-
lessly in the course of this. With a double or triple block on the boom
end, one or more of the falls of the sheet will always have a foul lead
from the block and will chafe itself to death. This will also greatly in-

crease the friction in the tackle, and make sheeting in much more difficult.

Instead of using a multiple block, provide each fall of the sheet with its own single block, and these should be hung from bent shackles so they can turn into a comfortable position. For this reason, I designed my fitting with two lower arms, one for each sheet block. For use with a three part sheet, I should have used three arms. The decrease in friction is quite astonishing, especially when we sheet in the main for a jibe on a windy day.

The moral, and I think there is a moral to this incident, must be "pay a little less attention to whether or not things are done in the customary way, and a little more attention to whether or not they make sense."

RETURN TO A CUTTER RIG—
DESIGN FOR A BOWSPRIT

Many lovely old cruising cutters have been "modernized" into very mediocre sloops. *Viking "S"* was one of these, and soon after we bought her, I decided to restore the cutter rig for which she had been designed. The results have been most gratifying. She sails faster and more happily, she balances better, and the two smaller headsails make shorthanded sailing much less arduous.

When I designed the bowsprit for this conversion, I attempted to design the entire "front end" of the rig as a unit. It has worked out very well in every respect. All the foredeck functions were provided for in the original design, rather than adding chain rollers, fairleads, and tack fittings after the bowsprit was in place. As you can see from Figure 21, there is a wide comfortable area on which to stand provided by the top of the bowsprit and the two planks which run along its sides. These are covered with non-skid plastic deck covering, which gives a very secure footing, even in bad weather.

The cranse iron incorporates the attachments for the bowsprit shrouds, bobstay, and headstay as well as a sheave for the jib tack downhaul. This fitting was built up from stainless steel plate 4 millimeters thick. The sheave was turned from bronze with a groove to fit the stainless wire I used for the downhaul whip, and turns on a stain-

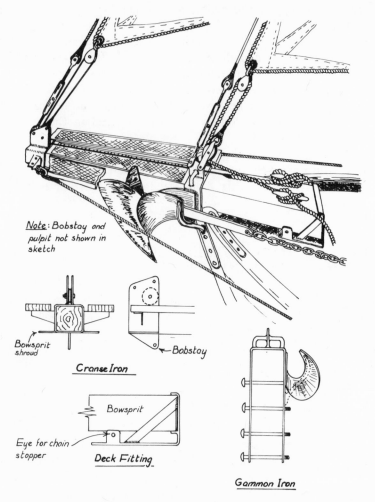

Fig. 21—Bowsprit design for Viking "S."

less steel pin. Two angle brackets of lighter stainless steel were welded on to support the forward ends of the two planks or duckboards. The after ends of these are held by stainless angles screwed to the sides of the bowsprit itself.

The bowsprit was made from a select balk of spruce cut to a rectangular cross section. The width was established as exactly the width of the stem timber, so that the gammon iron could be a simple inverted "U" in shape. The forward section of the bowsprit tapers slightly, but abaft the gammon iron the cross section remains the same. This allows me to unship the bowsprit easily when I wish to paint the deck.

The gammon iron incorporates a fin to which the forestay is attached as well as an eye for the downhaul for the staysail tack, as shown in Figure 21. In addition, I welded on two "L" shaped pieces of ½ inch stainless steel rod to form sturdy eyes on either side of the fitting. These have proven very useful. I snap a large snap shackle snatch-block into one when I want a good chafe-free fairlead for the kedge warp. One of these eyes makes an ideal location for a swivel block for the main boom preventer which we keep set up when we are cruising. These eyes are strong enough to take any load I may ever wish to put on them, and are large enough to pass a large shackle easily.

On the port side of the gammon iron is the fairlead for the main anchor, which is a CQR. I have seldom seen a chain roller that was not seized up from rust, and even less frequently have I seen one large enough in diameter to serve as anything other than an impediment to the chain passing over it. I decided, instead of a roller, to employ a large flaring horn shape of stainless plate, and I have been delighted by its performance. The radius over which the chain passes is quite large in any direction, and the lead is just as fair with the chain leading off to the side as it is from straight ahead. There is never any need for cleaning or oiling, and this same fitting stows the anchor when we are under way. I simply tighten the chain, pulling the anchor firmly back into the horn, and it rides very well without even being lashed down. A small stainless strip on the rail cap takes the wear when the chain is running out, and a brace made from ½ inch stainless rod supports the outboard side of the horn against the extreme strain it sometimes has to bear.

The deck fitting supports the heel of the bowsprit two inches above the deck to allow us to clean underneath it. The angle braces, welded in place, serve to confine the bowsprit laterally, and the two lips engaging its upper and lower surfaces restrict its vertical motion. This fitting is set in bedding compound, held in place by four ½ inch stainless steel through bolts, and is backed up by a 2 inch oak block across the deck beams below. This makes it sufficiently secure to carry the eye to which the chain stopper is secured, and to which we ride when we are at anchor, thus taking the strain off the anchor windlass. This fitting could also carry the swivel pedestal for a staysail boom, but I happen to prefer a loose footed staysail.

These fittings could be made from bronze or from galvanized steel, but stainless is not so much more expensive since it can be much lighter than bronze for equivalent strength. Its appearance and freedom from maintenance problems would seem to more than justify its use. A bowsprit arrangement of this type, together with a nice pulpit (not shown in the illustration for the sake of clarity) will do more than make you proud of your yacht's appearance. They will also add immeasurably to your pleasure and comfort in working the foredeck, and greatly add to the safety of your cruising.

SAFE FOOTING ALOFT

If one has rattled shrouds, the lower spreaders make a very convenient station for a lookout, and from this vantage point one can often raise a light which might not be visible for another two or three hours at deck level. A lookout aloft is able to see submerged hazards much better than from the deck, and is at a tremendous advantage when trying to locate something which has gone adrift.

To adapt your spreaders for this purpose, you must first secure them so they will bear the load. This may be done by running light wire lifts to the next higher mast fitting, splicing the lower ends into small eyebolts running through the ends of the spreaders. No adjustment for tension is needed if the lifts are carefully made to length. If you do not like the idea of extra rigging aloft, put a heavy wire seizing or "mouse" on the shroud just below the spreader and let this take the load. If your spreader is not already seized to the shroud, you can do this neatly with a small stainless steel strap run around the end of the spreader and held on each side with two wood screws. (See Figure 22.)

Now for the upper surface of the spreader. The usual paint or varnish is a deadly thing to stand on if it is wet from mist or spray. I have found that a narrow strip of textured plastic or rubber non-skid deck covering is ideal for this purpose. Make sure the spreader surface is well painted or varnished first, then sand the last coat and cement

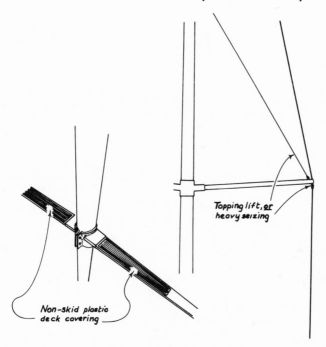

Fig. 22—Safe footing aloft.

the material in place with a contact cement. Augment this with copper tacks around the edges of the material, since the alternate wetting and drying seems to loosen the material if one relies on the cement alone.

Now, when one of your crew scrambles aloft, you needn't be so concerned about his safety, and when you order someone aloft he will go more willingly. Make sure he wears a good safety harness, however. With this secured to the mast above the spreader, he certainly will not get into any serious difficulty.

A WALKWAY ON THE BOWSPRIT

Even with a good pulpit and a short bowsprit, changing a jib in heavy weather can be a trying experience. Most of the difficulty is due to the insecure footing offered by the average bowsprit. A great improvement can be made by applying a strip of non-skid deck covering to the upper surface of the bowsprit, cementing it on with contact cement and then tacking the edges with copper tacks.

A further improvement consists of attaching a length of plank to the bowsprit to provide a flat walkway. It need not be very wide— six inches is ample—but it too should be given some non-skid finish. I like the plastic deck material for this, but non-skid deck paint or enamel or varnish sprinkled with sharp dry sand will do very well. (See Figure 23.)

Arthur Roca has suggested that the ideal walkway for a bowsprit would be V-shaped, so that one side or the other would be more or less horizontal when the boat is heeled over. This is a very provocative idea, and sounds well worth developing. After all, it is while going to weather that one is usually most threatened by insecure footing on the bowsprit, and this is also when the greatest angle of heel is present.

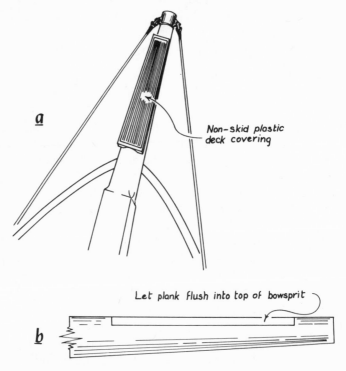

_a_

Non-skid plastic deck covering

Let plank flush into top of bowsprit

_b_

Fig. 23—Walkway on bowsprit.

No man works well on the foredeck when his primary concern is for his own survival. The more you can do to make your foredeck crew feel secure, the more they will give you in the way of fast and effective sail handling.

PULPITS FOR USE WITH BOWSPRITS

It seems to me that the real function of a pulpit is seldom thought through by the people who design them, since pulpits too often turn out to be merely things which a man can hold on to. Especially in a cruising yacht, this definition does not go far enough. The pulpit must actually serve to support a man securely *so that he can work effectively in all sorts of weather.* Many small low pulpits will help to keep a man from going overboard if he sits on deck and holds on with both hands, and on a very small, sloop-rigged boat this is certainly better than putting to sea with no pulpit at all. On such a boat, a man can actually work the jib reasonably well sitting down. The most glaring deficiencies in design are to be seen on cutters and on yawls and ketches which carry bowsprits. Eric Hiscock, in his *Cruising Under Sail,*[*] even goes so far as to say "Unfortunately, a pulpit cannot conveniently be arranged aboard a yacht with a bowsprit . . ."

This, of course, is utter nonsense. It is true that one cannot often stop by the "handy corner chandlery" and buy, out of stock, a pulpit which can be fitted without modification to a boat with a bowsprit, but there is no reason to assume that one cannot be designed and made to function perfectly well. As a matter of fact, many of the best designed pulpits I have seen have been on boats which did carry bowsprits.

The usual shortcoming is insufficient height. This is always explained as being necessary to avoid interfering with the foot of the staysail, but height this far aft is not necessary nor even particularly desirable. The height is needed out on the bowsprit between the forestay and the jibstay where a man can wedge himself in place while working the jib. Figure 24a shows a rather typical pulpit installation in a yacht with a bowsprit. It is too low to offer much security, and

---

[*] Eric Hiscock, *Cruising Under Sail* (2nd ed., New York: Oxford University Press, Inc., 1965).

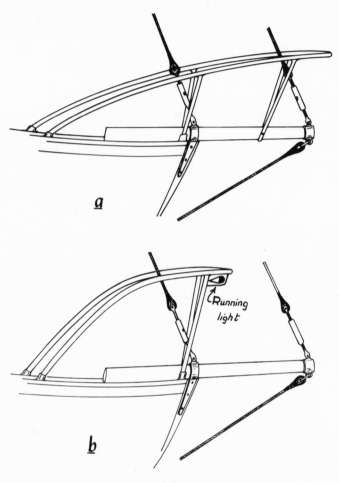

Fig. 24—*Pulpit design.*

it is rather difficult to brace rigidly. Much of this latter defect arises because of the unnecessary length of the pulpit.

There is no need for the pulpit to run forward of the jibstay. Actually, the man working the jib will get much more secure support from a pulpit such as that shown in Figure 24b, which stops short of the jibstay. He can lean against the forward curve of the pulpit and be just within easy reach of the stay to remove or to hank on a sail. The height, at the forward end of the pulpit, should be sufficient to support the man *at his hips,* and the width should be just sufficient to allow him to wedge himself in. With a pulpit of this design, the crewman will feel sufficiently secure to get his work done in half the time.

Because of its shorter length, this type of pulpit can be made more rigid with fewer stanchions and braces, and can be kept sufficiently low abaft the stemhead to eliminate any interference with the staysail foot. It is also protected from damage. During storms, I have often seen yachts drag their anchors or moorings and come down on other boats. Very frequently the pulpit is the first point of contact, and, of course, it is always damaged as a result. The heavy bowsprit, on the other hand, is capable of taking much more punishment of this kind. It usually does so anyway, after the pulpit has been mangled.

If you are contemplating the installation of a pulpit, you might consider mounting your running lights on it. The wires can be led through the tubing of the pulpit, if you wish to make a first class job, and the lights will be located in a position where they cannot be blanketed by a headsail. You will also find that the helmsman has better night visibility if the running lights are forward where none of their light is reflected from the sails and deck.

III
DECK FITTINGS

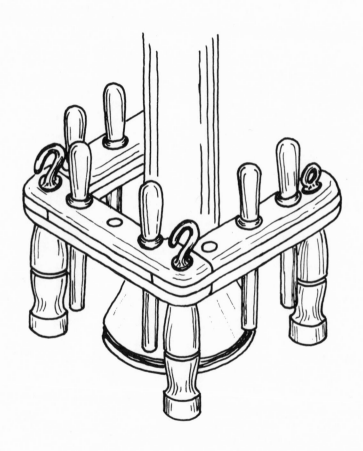

A PROPER PIN RAIL

When we bought *Viking* "S," she had a galvanized rail with the pins welded in place. It was something of an eyesore, and it played havoc with the halyards, since the pins were too small and the galvanized finish was extremely abrasive. I designed and made the pin rail shown here to replace the original one. It has proven to be very practical, easy on the halyards, and a very attractive addition to our deck. Since I had very limited shop facilities at the time I made this, the design is one which avoids the need for difficult joinery.

The rail itself is made from three thicknesses of hardwood. I used ash, but nearly any hardwood would do. The corners were lapped, as shown in the sketch (Figure 25), and this avoided the need for cutting

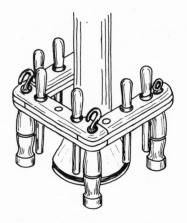

Fig. 25—Pinrail.

dovetails or mortises. The nine pieces were glued with resorcinol glue and clamped for twenty-four hours. The glued-up piece was then worked down, all the corners rounded, and finished with fine sandpaper.

The spacing for the mounting bolts was determined by the location of the deck beams and mast partners, carefully laid out on paper, and then transferred to the pin rail. Holes for the mounting bolts were drilled, after which the holes for the belaying pins were located and drilled.

The mounting bolts were made of ½ inch stainless steel rods, long enough to pass through the deck and the beams beneath. I finished two of these bolts with eyes and two with hooks at the top instead of bolt heads, since I planned to use the hooks for belaying the headsail halyards (see page 16). Washers of ⅛ inch stainless steel were welded in place just below the hooks and the eyes, and the weld was turned down in a lathe to make a nice fillet.

The legs could be square and plain, and would be easier to maintain if they were. I managed to get access to a lathe, and couldn't resist the temptation to embellish them a bit. The upper end of the legs should terminate in a shoulder or round tenon, which fits into a 1½ inch hole bored halfway through the pin rail from beneath. Drill the legs to pass the mounting bolts, using a ship's auger with a long shank and being very careful to keep this hole centered as well as possible.

Using the paper pattern, lay out the mounting holes on the deck and drill them. Assemble the pin rail without glue, insert the mounting bolts, and try it in place. With all the legs well seated in the pin rail, spile around them with a pair of dividers which have been opened far enough to stay on wood all the way around all of the legs. Remove the pin rail and trim the legs to this spiled line. They should now fit perfectly against the deck.

Cut some washers from sheet lead just the size of the bottom face of the legs and with a hole to pass the mounting bolts. Now, having varnished the pin rail well, you are ready to mount it. Coat the tenons on the upper ends of the legs with glue and insert them into the holes in the rail. Pass the mounting bolts through the legs, and slide the lead washers in place after having coated each side of the lead with bedding compound. Insert the bolts in the holes in the deck and push the rail down to place.

Now, have someone hold the bolt heads to keep them from turning, and put on the nuts over good-sized washers. Take these up until the legs are firmly bedded against the deck and the glue joints at the top are fully closed. Then take them up some more. They want to be really well pulled down. Allow the glue to set, and then cut off the ends of the bolts below deck and smooth their ends with a file.

The belaying pins may be made from either wood or metal. Locust, ash, or hickory will do nicely, or they can be made from brass or bronze rod. The important thing is to make them large enough. Too small a diameter makes too sharp a nip in the halyards and tends to break the fibers. Too short a pin often means you haven't enough room for belaying turns. If you soak the wood in hot oil for a few hours, you can omit varnish which rapidly gets worn off the pins by the halyards. This oiling should be repeated once in a while to keep the wood from checking too much.

COMBINATION MOORING BITT AND VENTILATOR

Mooring bitts are usually too small and too weakly fastened to be as useful as they might be. The bitts shown here are large enough to do a real job, and they serve the very welcome secondary function of providing ventilation for spaces which ordinarily are not too well supplied with fresh air. This dual function keeps your decks more free from assorted fittings and offers fewer things to foul lines or trip you up at night.

This bitt is made from large size pipe, bronze or stainless steel if you are lucky enough to be able to find it. An eight inch length of four inch diameter pipe will do for the average yacht. Ordinary steel pipe can be used, of course, but it does rust and is very difficult to maintain, even if it is galvanized. Square up the ends of this pipe in the lathe, and drill the holes for the cross bar. This is made from one inch pipe if you can find it with thick walls, or from rod stock if there is any doubt about the strength of the pipe available. Weld the cross bar in place and finish the joints.

Cut a disk to fit the top of the post and weld it in place. Smooth and polish this joint to a nice rounded edge. Lay out the ring of air intake holes and cut these out. They are more easily cut square as shown on the drawing (Figure 26) but it is well to round the upper outside edges with a file to eliminate chafe on mooring lines. These holes should be kept down where they will be clear of mooring lines so far as possible. Smooth the edges of all the holes and cut three or four drains as shown.

Make the base from heavy plate stock, and bore it for the intake tube. This tube should be about two inches in diameter if you have used four inch pipe. Its walls may be quite thin, although if they are too thin it will make the welding difficult. Cut this tube to length so that its upper end will be at least an inch above the air intake ports and its lower end will extend through the deck planking and the oak pad which should be used to back up the deck planks in the way of

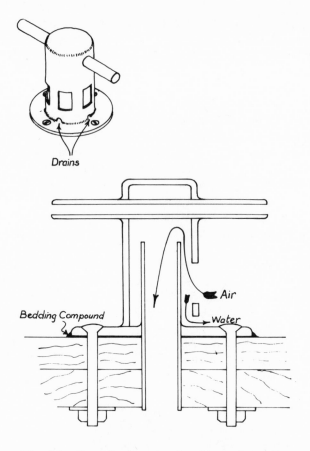

Drains

Air

Water

Bedding Compound

Fig. 26—Combination mooring bit and ventilator.

this bitt. Locate the air intake tube in the base plate and weld it in place. Round the edges of the base plate, and drill and countersink it for the mounting bolts. Place the post with its cross arm on the base plate, and when it is correctly centered, weld it securely.

With the oak pad in place below the planking, bore a hole for the air intake tube, making it an easy slide fit. Insert the fitting and mark the location of the four mounting holes. The mounting bolts should be $\frac{5}{16}$ inch if you are using stainless steel or $\frac{3}{8}$ inch if you use bronze. Don't even try to use brass bolts. They are not suitable for this kind of application.

Liberally coat the underside of the base plate with bedding compound and seat the fitting on the deck. Coat the bolts with bedding compound, drive them through, and set them up with washers, lock washers, and nuts.

Ideally I'd like six of these fittings on my boat; two on the foredeck, two on the afterdeck, and one on each side amidships. One can always use good substantial bitts in these locations, and the added ventilation would be very welcome.

EXTENSION FOR SHEET WINCH HANDLE

Some of the larger sizes of ungeared sheet winches are engineered to withstand far more stress than can be applied with the short handles provided. At best, they are no substitutes for geared winches when it comes to handling larger headsails in a real blow, but geared winches are expensive and this modification does a good job of narrowing the gap if your winch mountings are secure enough to take the added strain.

A length of pipe of suitable diameter is formed at one end to allow it to slide over the end of the winch handle. It is then pinched sufficiently to prevent its sliding on farther than the desired distance. Eight or nine inches of overlap is enough.

The pipe is cut off to the desired length. Mine just doubles the original handle length, and of course this just doubles the power of the winch. The ends are smoothed and the pipe is painted or hot dipped, unless you have used stainless steel in which case a good polishing is all that will ever be needed. The end of the handle should be served with marline to provide a secure grip. (See Figure 27.)

Since this extension is needed only in strong winds and with certain

Fig. 27—Extension handle for sheet winch.

sails, I carry it in a special rack where it is out of the way unless it is actually needed. It may be slipped in place over the regular handle in a matter of seconds.

If your winch handle is the type with a crank handle at the end, such as the Merriman pattern bottom-acting winches use, it is worth making up a second handle for the extension. The crank end can be cut off, and the flattened pipe section permanently fastened to it with bolts or rivets.

With this extension, even my wife who is a real flyweight can make the winch do its job in all but the worst weather. We also use it frequently to give us a little help in warping in to a dock or in taking up on a taut stern line during a storm in harbor.

ROLLER JAM CLEATS FOR HEADSAIL SHEETS

Tacking or even just flattening a headsail in heavy weather can demand a nice bit of timing. Even with the two-part sheets we use in lieu of winches it is necessary to luff momentarily in order to get the staysail really flat, and this gives only a few seconds in which to get the sheet in and belay it before we must bear away to keep way on.

This cleat takes most of the guesswork out of the maneuver. Mounted on the outside of the cockpit coaming (suitably reinforced) as shown in Figure 28c, it allows the sheet to run freely on the sheave when the direction of pull is slightly aft of the vertical. As soon as the hauling end of the sheet is swung forward a short distance, it jams in the jaws of the cleat with no danger of its slipping before it can be belayed. The same type of cleat can be mounted on the side deck if a wedge-shaped pad or mounting block is made to give the sheet a lead from which one can haul comfortably and effectively. In either case the cleat should be firmly bolted to place rather than relying on wood screws to hold it.

Any hard, close grained wood can be used for these cleats. Locust is excellent and ash makes a very strong and attractive cleat. Lay out the pattern after having bought the sheaves required. These should be of bronze and should be fitted with roller bearings. For ½ inch or $\frac{9}{16}$ inch diameter sheets, the sheave diameter should be no less than 2½ inches. The jamming jaws should be carefully planned in terms of the sheets for which they are intended. The sheet should jam in the

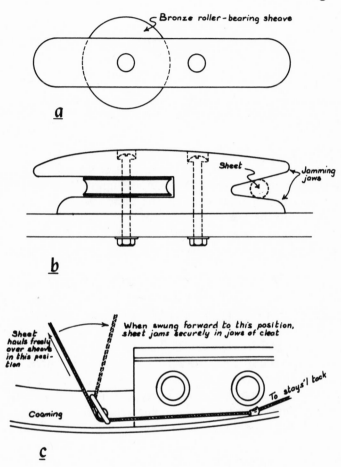

Fig. 28—*Roller-type jam cleat for sheets.*

jaws well before it reaches the bottom of the "Vee," as shown in Figure 28b. Either saw out the swallow for the sheave, or laminate the cleat with a good resorcinol glue, in which case the swallow can be cut out of the center lamination before gluing up.

All edges should be nicely rounded, but the jamming jaws themselves should have relatively flat faces in order to grip the sheet over a broad area rather than just at one point. Sand the cleats well and varnish them before you mount them. The mounting bolts should be chosen of a diameter to fit the bearing hole in the sheave, and the holes should be counter-bored to set the heads below the level of the top of the cleat. The axle hole should not be plugged after the cleat is mounted as you will wish to remove this bolt from time to time to grease the sheave bearing. You can plug the other bolt hole if you wish, but if they are left open the cleats may be removed easily from time to time for greasing and revarnishing. The bolt heads should have screwdriver slots so you can hold them while setting up the nuts.

You will find that cleats of this type make sheet handling a pleasure. By swinging the end of the sheet aft, one can ease out just an inch or two and never lose control, since a slight shift forward jams the sheet instantly. The belay is easily accomplished by taking a hitch over the protruding lower horn of the cleat. When hauling in, the sheet need never be taken off the cleat, but is always in position for instant snubbing. These cleats should work equally well for a main sheet, where the belaying problems in a hard blow can be even more trying.

PLASTIC COVERED WIRE FOR LIFELINES

Plastic covered wire rope can be had for just a fraction of the cost of stainless, or even of good galvanized wire for that matter, and properly handled it can serve quite adequately for lifelines. As a matter of fact, I have seen several cruising boats which used this material for lower shrouds and backstays and topping lifts, and I can see no reason why it should not be all right for any application in which chafe is not a factor.

Since the wire rope inside the plastic covering is not even galvanized, the successful use of this material depends entirely on keeping moisture out of the splices whch have to be made at the ends. I have seen some lifelines in which the eye was simply seized in and served over, and the owners say that these have held up very well. I still prefer to have eyes that are spliced in, and the method shown in the illustrations has worked very well for this. One nice thing about the clear plastic covering is the ability to see any rust which begins to form on the wire. After three seasons of use, my lifelines still show no rust at all in the splices.

Select a wire of sufficient strength for the purpose, and buy thimbles to fit the plastic covering. The last wire I used was made up of five strands. This splices very easily, and can be had in sizes that offer more than adequate strength along with a diameter that is comfortable to the hand. Cut the plastic off the end of the wire for a distance of about ten inches. Unlay the wire, and if the strands show any tendency to unlay, whip them or tape them.

Bend the wire around the thimble and mark the exact length required to go around and just meet at the throat. *This length of plastic will be left on the wire.* Remove the plastic for another 3½ inches beyond this point (see Figure 29a). The splice will be made in this section.

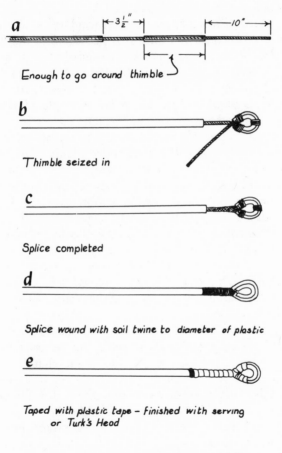

Fig. 29—Waterproof eye splice for lifelines.

Seize the center of the thimble in the center of the covered portion of wire. Bend the ends around one at a time and seize them as near the throat of the thimble as possible. A small amount of the plastic should project beyond the ends of the thimble on each side as in Figure 29b.

Now splice the eye, using any method you wish for the tucking. See the article on Wire Splicing on page 162 if you are in doubt about this. It will not be necessary to taper the splice, so don't waste time on this. Three tucks in each strand should be sufficient. Cut off the ends of the strands and work the splice down smooth with a pair of pliers. It should now look like Figure 29c.

Serve the splice with sail twine, "scatter winding" it to build up the diameter of the spliced section until it is just equal to the diameter of the plastic covered portion of the wire beyond the splice, as shown in Figure 29d. Now tape the splice with plastic electrician's tape. Start at the eye and tape one leg first, stretching the tape as you apply it, to get it as tight as possible. Be sure to lay a couple of layers tightly across the throat of the eye. Cut off the tape and start on the other leg, taping down to the throat and then over the served portion and for another two inches onto the undisturbed plastic covering. Cut the tape off and serve it neatly with some fishline or small marline. This is necessary, because no matter how securely the end of the tape seems to have adhered, it will come loose in a short time and begin to unwrap. The finished job should look like Figure 29e.

If you have taped the splice carefully, it should be waterproof and should last at least as long as mine have. The tough plastic covering left on the wire forming the eye is sufficient protection against chafe from the thimble. This section may be served before turning in the splice if your thimbles are unusually rough or sharp, but ordinarily this is not necessary.

Used in this way, the plastic covered wire should make good and very inexpensive standing rigging. It could not be used for stays on which sails are to be set, nor for shrouds where chafe from headsail sheets cannot be entirely eliminated, but in other applications it should be quite all right. I have recently seen this wire with white and colored opaque plastic covering. I should avoid this like the plague, since it is the ability to see rust beginning to form which makes the transparent type so practical and safe.

IV
ENGINES AND MACHINERY

IMPROVISED PUMP LEATHERS

We attempt to keep a good supply of spares on board, but it is impossible to have duplicates of everything. I now have a stock of pump leathers among the spares, but twice I have had a fresh water pump fail at sea because of a worn out leather and been unable to locate any replacements. On these occasions I managed to improvise quite serviceable leathers, and the method seems worth passing on.

Cut a leather disk from some scrap leather. I usually have some aboard, but in a pinch a piece cut from an old shoe would do nicely. Try the metal plunger in the pump barrel, and notice the amount of space available for the leather. This will help you to select the proper thickness of leather. Make the diameter of the leather disk equal to the diameter of the metal plunger plus twice its height. Cut or punch a hole in the center of the leather to pass the screw or stud which holds the leather in place as shown in Figure 30a.

Soak the leather disk in water until it becomes soft and pliable. It will help if the water is warm, and if a little detergent is added. When the leather is thoroughly soaked, blot off the excess moisture and secure the leather to the metal plunger by the screw and washer or the stud, depending upon the type of pump you have.

Now work the edges of the leather down over the sides of the metal plunger with your hand, smoothing out the wrinkles that form at the edge and moulding the leather as closely as possible to the metal, as shown in Figure 30b. Adjust a hose clamp to a size that will just permit you to slide it down over the leather cup you have formed as in Figure 30c. Tighten the screw of the hose clamp, drawing the leather skirt tightly against the sides of the metal plunger. Leave the hose clamp in place until the leather has dried. This may be hastened by setting it on deck in the sun, but do not attempt to heat it to dry it.

Remove the clamp, trim the edges of the leather, and you will find that you have a very adequate replacement leather and that your galley is back in business. You can expect the leather to be a bit tight when you first try the pump, but it will loosen with a little use.

I especially like this method, since there are always hose clamps aboard a cruising boat. If there are no spares, you can always take one out of service for the time needed to make the pump leather. I am not

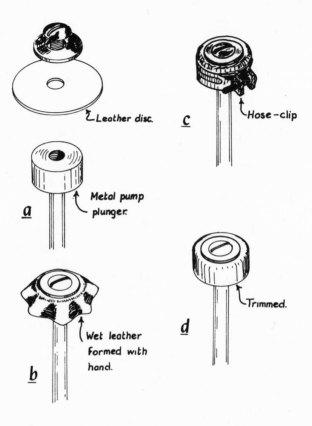

Fig. 30—*Improvised pump leathers.*

suggesting this as a substitute for a properly stocked spares cupboard, but it will get your pump working again in a pinch, and a cruising boat without fresh water is not a particularly happy ship.

A CONTROL CABLE YOU CAN MAKE

While installing an engine in a French port, I discovered that the supplier had failed to ship a cable for the stopping control. A canvass of the local shops failed to produce anything that could be adapted satisfactorily, so I looked through my stock of spares to see what I had to work with. I found some ³⁄₃₂ inch flexible stainless steel halyard wire which I had bought to rig a sailing dinghy, and with it an end terminal of the "chuck type" which can be attached very securely by screwing down a cone-shaped collet.

I put an eye splice in one end of the wire, as shown in Figure 31, and left the other end long to be cut to length later. Copper tubing was locally available, so I bought a length of six millimeter (¼ inch) tubing long enough to reach to the control in easy curving bends. One end of this tubing was soldered to a brass bracket which was screwed to the inside of a bulkhead where the control knob was to be located.

I had some ¼ inch brass shafting aboard, so I bent a hook at one end of this to take the eye splice in the wire, forming the hook so that it could be moused to hold the eye in place. This brass rod was passed

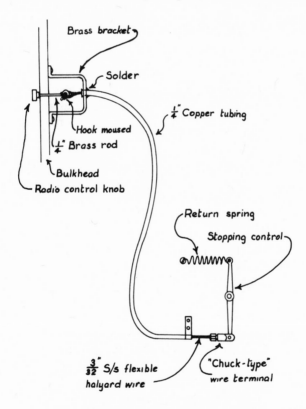

Fig. 31—Control cable you can make.

through a ¼ inch hole in the hard wood of the bulkhead. In soft wood, I should have tubed the hole to prevent wear.

Knowing that most radio controls have ¼ inch shafts, I went to a radio repair shop and bought a simple round control knob with a brass bushing and a setscrew. This made a very acceptable control knob when mounted on the end of the brass rod, which was drilled for the end of the setscrew to provide a very secure attachment of the knob.

The other end of the copper tubing was soldered to a brass strap which, in turn, was bolted to the side of the fuel pump housing. The tubing was bent carefully to avoid any buckling and the end of the tubing was pointed at the end of the stopping control lever.

The patent wire terminal had a hole of just the right size to take the bolt in the end of the control lever, so it was attached at this point. The stainless wire was carefully cut to the right length and clamped firmly in the collet of the fitting, after being coated with a little Molyslip.

A coil return spring was attached to the other end of the control lever to return it to the "run" position, and the control was complete. A slight pull on the radio knob draws the flexible wire through the copper tubing and operates the control. As soon as it is released, the control is returned to the "run" position by the spring. It has worked smoothly and effectively for two years now—more than I can say for most of the control cables I have bought.

This type of control will work very well for any application calling for a "pull," and in which the "push" movement of the cable can be replaced by spring tension. It seems to be ideal for stopping controls on diesel engines, remote control of hatch locks or latches, searchlight aiming controls, and any intermittent use. I should not recommend its use where there will be more or less constant movement of the cable through the tubing, such as would be the case in wind-vane steering gears, etc. I think in such cases there would be excessive wear of the copper sheath.

DRAINS FOR SELF-BAILING COCKPIT

The cockpit in most cruising yachts is far too large for optimum safety in ocean sailing. The Tahiti Ketch with its tiny well for the helmsman's feet and its seats actually at deck level is certainly safer,

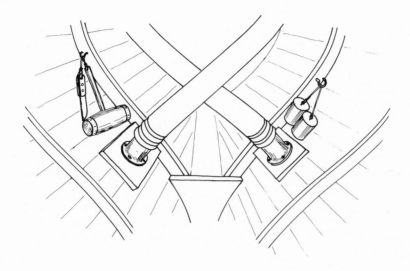

Fig. 32—Drains for self-bailing cockpit.

but hardly as comfortable, either for sailing or for lying in harbor. Since nearly everything about a cruising yacht is a compromise, I suppose there is no reason why this should not be, but consider for a moment the matter of safety in really rough weather.

It is not unusual for a cruising yacht thirty feet overall to have a cockpit seven feet long, five feet wide and two and a half feet deep. Allowing for the space taken out for the cockpit seats, this still leaves a volume of some fifty-six cubic feet of water which could be dumped into the cockpit if the yacht is pooped. This volume of sea water weighs nearly thirty-six hundred pounds, and is located well above the center of buoyancy of the hull.

Assuming that the mean height of this volume is two feet above the outlets of the cockpit drains, and that the drains are one inch bore, the velocity of flow through the drains will be 3.9 feet per second. This is equivalent to 1.28 cubic feet per minute. With two such drains in operation, the draining time for the cockpit would be approximately twenty minutes.

Twenty minutes is an eternity to spend in a gale with seas high enough to have filled the cockpit. With this amount of added weight located where it is, the yacht is almost certain to be pooped again before the cockpit can have emptied itself. Consider also the fact that the cockpit is very seldom water-tight. The companionway slide and the openings for the engine controls will leak appreciably, and in twenty minutes quite a volume of water will have poured into the boat and over the engine. If repeated pooping does occur, the constant ingress of water will be more than the average bilge pump can keep pace with.

With drains of two inch bore, the expected flow would be 11.75 cubic feet per minute (for two such drains), and 19.8 cubic feet per minute with two and one-half inch drains. These calculations are based on the formula $V = C\sqrt{\dfrac{hD}{4 + 54D}}$, where C is a constant allowing for the fluid friction. Why, then are such larger drains so seldom seen in cockpits? The most reasonable explanation seems to be the high cost of sea cocks in the larger sizes. Is this additional cost, though, important enough to justify defeating the very purpose of a self-bailing cockpit installation?

If one really cannot afford the larger size of sea cocks, he might do well to consider this proposal. Eliminate the sea cocks, and run the oversize drain hoses directly to the through-hull fitting. Make up several tapered wooden plugs of a size that will just fit the hull fitting, and hang these by lanyards together with a stainless steel knife and a mallet, from a hook near the hull fittings. (See Figure 32.) Cutting the hose with the knife and driving in a plug should take no more time than closing the average sea cock—perhaps less, and the result should be just as secure and positive.

This arrangement would have one additional advantage. The effect of the presence of a fully open gate valve in a pipe is to reduce the pressure head as much as a length of pipe equal to six diameters. Thus the system without sea cocks should drain significantly faster than the same system with sea cocks. Note also that all these calculations are based on the assumption that the drains are layed out with no sharp bends and that they are clean and free from undue roughness throughout their bore. This type of layout will make it very easy to run a swab through the drains a few times a season, as well as to clear them rapidly if they should become clogged during use.

GALVANIC CORROSION IN HYDRAULIC LINES

Eight months after installing a new engine with a hydraulically operated gear box I began to have trouble with the hydraulic system. The controls would go out (and that can be somewhat embarrassing in a busy harbor), and I would spend the next day bleeding the system and checking for leaks, but not finding any. After this had happened three or four times, I removed the hydraulic lines and gave them a careful looking over. Right where they had passed through the engine room overhead, under the cockpit seat, I found they had some deeply etched spots.

When I looked closely at the overhead I realized that it was lead-sheathed at this point. This was something I had not noticed previously, even when I bored the holes for the lines, as the lead was painted over. Examination of the lines showed that they were of soft steel tubing with a plating of what appeared to be cadmium. Of course there was a tremendous galvanic reaction between the lead and the steel as soon as the thin cadmium plating wore through, and in fact the the etched areas in the lines proved to be filled with pinhole size leaks.

I replaced the lines with copper tubing, sheathing this with plastic tubing where it passes through the lead, and have had no more trouble of this kind. The copper tubing is quite strong enough to withstand the pressure involved, and many times more resistant to corrosion. I don't know how universal this practice of using steel tubing for hydraulic lines has become. It is probably much more likely to be encountered if you buy an engine from a company that also manufactures truck engines. I would suggest, however, that you have a look at your hydraulic lines. You can easily tell if they are steel by holding a small magnetic compass next to them. If they are, the needle will be strongly deflected, in which case, either change them for a less easily corroded metal, or very carefully protect them from contact with any other metal less active than steel.

WORTHWHILE ADDITIONS TO YOUR TOOL KIT

Several common surgical instruments (Figure 33) are to be found in my tool kit and ditty bag, and I find that I am constantly using them for tasks which I could hardly accomplish without them. They can be obtained from a surgical or dental supply house, and they may very

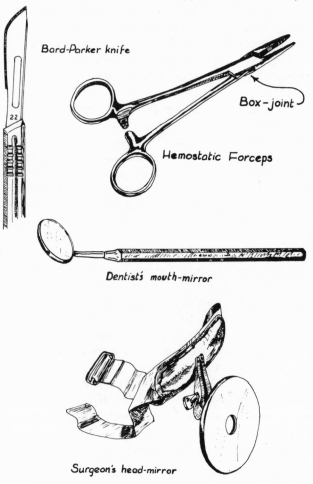

Fig. 33—*Worthwhile additions to your tool kit.*

well be available second hand. Ask about this, for used instruments will serve your purpose just as well and will cost far less than new ones.

Hemostatic Forceps. Be certain that these are stainless steel, and do not get the "mouse-tooth" or tissue-forcep type—plain serrated jaws are best. These are invaluable for retrieving small parts from inaccessible corners. Use them to clamp together pieces of canvas which you are sewing. They are faster and better than pins for this, and may be moved along as the work progresses. I use two pairs and leapfrog them one over the other as I sew. They are excellent for tying knots in short ends of cords, and are perfect for removing fish hooks. They make fine clamps for holding small parts for filing, assembling, or gluing, and are very handy for radio and instrument repairs. Clipped to the leads of a transistor, for example, they conduct away the heat when the connection is soldered and prevent damage to the transistor.

They are useful for fishing small objects out of drains, and they save wear and tear on your fingers if you use them to hold small tacks or brads when you are driving them in tight corners. With a lanyard attached to the handles, a pair of these makes a fine bench hook for sail-making and general canvas sewing. Since they can be clipped to the material, there is no need to depend upon a seam into which a hook may be inserted.

These forceps are made in two ways, as far as the joint is concerned. Try to get the type with the box joint rather than the lap joint. They last much longer and never become loose and sloppy in the joint. In stainless steel they hardly ever need any attention beyond a drop of oil once a year to keep the joint free.

Dentist's mouth mirror. This is extremely useful when you have to "see around a corner." It is small and can be tucked into most places to give you a glimpse of what has to be done, or of where your fingers are at the moment. Again, get a stainless steel handle, and a *plane* mirror about ⅞ inch in diameter. Concave mirrors are available, but don't try them. They are tricky to use. They must be held at the proper distance to focus properly and, since they magnify, they do strange things to the perspective. The mirrors are replaceable and will get scratched up eventually, so it isn't a bad idea to get a spare.

Surgeon's Head Mirror. This is a concave mirror about three inches in diameter which is attached by a ball and socket joint to a leather or cloth tape head band. There is a small hole in the center of the mirror through which you look with one eye, while the other eye looks past the edge of the mirror. Get the salesman to check you out on this. The mirror, itself, is used to reflect the light from a lamp onto your work. This item is a mechanic's dream, since it lets you direct a beam of light down any deep narrow hole while you are looking *down the center of the light beam.* You can get perfect illumination *and* visibility into deep stud holes, pipes, bearings, and countless other places where otherwise you have to choose between being able to see into a dark hole *or* to shine a light into a hole where you can't see. You also get the bonus of having both hands free for your work.

Bard-Parker knives. These are surgical scalpels with stainless steel handles and replaceable blades. They will do the same jobs as an Exacto knife, but the stainless handles do not succumb to the salt air on a boat. The blades are carbon steel, but come in a paper packet in which they show little tendency to rust. I prefer the No. 4 handle and the No. 22 blade for most things, but look them over and choose what appeals to you. They will assure you of having a truly razor-sharp knife on hand at all times, and some of the blades are ideal for cutting gaskets, leather washers, pump leathers, etc. If you have any rust problem with the blades, store them in a small plastic vial full of light oil.

V
INSTRUMENTS AND
ELECTRICAL SYSTEMS

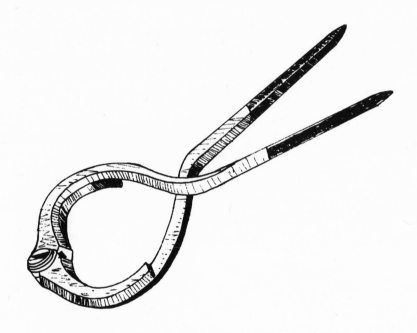

A SIGNAL SYSTEM FOR THE HELMSMAN

On cruises, the helmsman is frequently alone on deck, and this is especially likely to be the case during the night watches. He does need help, from time to time, to roll in a reef or to hand a sail, and this need often arises out of circumstances which make it difficult or impossible for him to leave the helm to turn someone out. Many skippers leave standing orders to be called under certain circumstances, but these very circumstances often make it difficult or dangerous for the helmsman to leave his station to do this.

The problem can be solved very nicely by mounting a set of waterproof push button switches in the cockpit and using these to sound strategically located bells or buzzers (Figure 34). One buzzer may be placed at the head of the skipper's berth and another in the passage berth where the next relief watch sleeps. Located properly, these need not be very loud in order to wake the man desired without disturbing the rest of the crew.

A third switch can operate a very loud bell located in the main saloon and used only in cases of real emergency when it is imperative

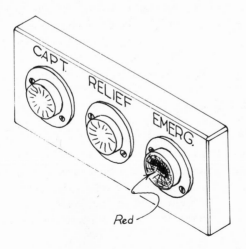

Fig. 34—A signal system for the helmsman.

to have all hands on deck as fast as possible. This switch can be painted red and set apart from the others to prevent any accidental sounding of the alarm. If you want to make *certain* that it is not set off unintentionally, use two switches connected in series and set a few inches apart. Both of these must be depressed at the same time to ring the alarm.

An interesting psychological by-product of such a system is that the helmsman actually seems to call for help less frequently. This is probably because he knows he can get immediate help whenever he really needs it, and that he needn't wonder whether his shouts have been heard below.

I have often been tempted to rig a buzzer on the foredeck to enable the helmsman to signal the foredeck crew. In a howling gale it is all but impossible to shout orders across this distance, and some sort of signalling system could be very useful.

ENGINE ROOM LAMP

In most sailboats the term "engine room" is somewhat of a euphemism, but regardless of what you call it, the space around the engine is much more useful if it can be well illuminated when the engine needs attention. All too often, after inserting himself into a space almost large enough to hold an unusually athletic cat, the yachtsman finds he needs both hands for the job to be done *and* an extra hand to hold a light. Working on my own I went through this routine many times with the usual results—balancing the flashlight on the manifold, maneuvering the injector into place, reaching for the wrench (always just out of reach directly behind me), seeing the light begin to move as the boat rolls, grabbing for the light and hearing the wrench tumble merrily into the bilge. After going through this I was driven to working out a solution for the problem and here it is. (See Figure 35.)

Most automobile supply houses sell "trouble lights" to be connected to the cigarette lighter socket, and these usually come equipped with a spring clamp which can be used to attach the light to any convenient support. Get one of these, remove the lighter socket connector and cut the wire to a length which will easily reach to any part of your engine compartment.

Next, stop at an office supply shop and buy one of the helical plastic

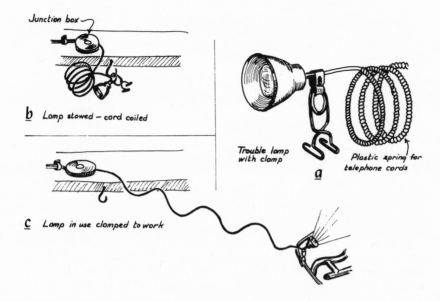

Fig. 35—Engine room lamp.

springs which are used to make a telephone cord "self-stowing." Work this plastic spring over the lamp cord and cut off any surplus that remains. Connect the lamp, by means of a junction box, to one of your lighting circuits and mount it on a bulkhead or beam alongside a large screw hook from which it may be hung. Of course you will have to provide a switch for the light in some convenient place.

The lamp can now be pulled out to any desired point and clipped onto the engine or some other point of support. The clamp will keep it pointed where you want it, and the cord will keep it out of the bilge, even if the clamp should slip off its support. When you are finished, the plastic helix coils the wire neatly for you and the lamp can be stowed so as to be instantly ready for the next job.

WATERPROOF BATTERY COVER

One ordinarily wishes to mount the storage batteries as low in the hull as possible in the interest of stability. If this is done, they are drowned very quickly if water accumulates in the bilge, and this immediately puts the electric bilge pump out of operation and creates starting problems with many main engines. This battery cover works on the principle of the old-fashioned diving bell, and enables you to have your batteries low in the bilge and still keep them dry and serviceable, even if they are covered by a considerable amount of water.

If you hold a. drinking glass upside down and push it down into a bowl of water, you will see the water rise only a little way inside the glass. The air above the water compresses only slightly and keeps the water from filling the inside of the glass. This cover, made from a heavy plastic tool bin, works in just this same fashion, and also protects the battery from any drip from the overhead. I have seen rectangular plastic basins that would work just as well.

Prepare a battery mount on a shelf or other horizontal surface, using wooden strips around the battery to keep it from sliding. Paint this mount with asphaltum varnish or other acid proof paint. Be certain that your battery cables have good waterproof insulation and if there is any doubt about this, replace them. Invert the plastic bin over the battery as shown in Figure 36, and secure it with a plastic covered wire strop and a pelican hook. This will hold the battery and cover in place, but makes it easy to get at the battery to service it.

Be sure to allow some open space around the lower edges of the plastic cover. Gases will be formed when the battery is charging, and you must make some provision for their escape. Bring the battery cables out under the edges of the cover, and then up to a connecting

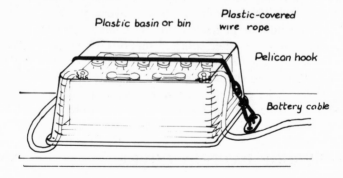

Fig. 36—Waterproof battery cover.

block located well above the water line. Try to keep the rest of the electrical system out of the bilges.

With a battery installation such as this, one can start and operate an electric bilge pump with two or three feet of water above the battery, and this could very well turn the tide if one were in trouble. I have known of several yachts which were lost because the crews were unable to keep up with the pumping by hand *and* repair the leak at the same time. If one can preserve the integrity of the electrical system, one can rely on the electric pump for a long enough period to be able to make some emergency repairs.

HELMSMAN'S MASTER SWITCH FOR LIGHTS

Your night vision is vastly improved if all the lights above deck are turned off, and this is especially true when a very faint haze increases the scattered light from the running lights. In your own home port, this may not be so important, although even there you may suddenly think you see a floating timber or an unlighted boat ahead. It can be very important when you are in unfamiliar waters or when you are trying to establish the course of an approaching vessel and can't quite see its navigation lights.

If all the lights on deck are wired through a single master switch which is located within easy reach of the helmsman, he can flick them all off at once, have a look, and then turn them on again without having to fumble with several different switches to do so. This should include your navigation lights, steaming light, stern light, binnacle light, and if your galley or cabin lights throw any light on deck, it is well to include them on the same circuit. I have come very near to being run down at times by unlighted fishing boats which I could not make out at all until I had doused everything including the binnacle light.

TRANSISTOR POWER CONVERTORS
FOR 110 VOLTS

We now have 110 volt a.c. power aboard, and we have it with no noise and no maintenance problems at all. A transistorized invertor operates with 85 per cent efficiency to provide this from our 12 volt battery system. I have been very impressed with the performance of these units, and since as far as I know they are available from only one source, I'll identify them as the Heathkit Marine Power Convertor MP-10 (or MPW-10 if you prefer one already assembled). They are easy to assemble yourself and somewhat less expensive in kit form.

These units contain no moving parts, and consequently they are completely free from maintenance problems or deterioration due to wear. They should be mounted in a *freely ventilated space,* and should be protected from spray since some of the mounting hardware used is quite susceptible to rust. They will enable you to operate a shaver, vacuum cleaner, soldering iron, tape recorder, etc., and two of them can be used in parallel to operate an electric drill, small sander, and similar tools.

One of these units will operate four 40 watt fluorescent light fixtures. This will give you more light for the current consumed than any other arrangement, and will all but eliminate the problem of burned out bulbs, since the tubes last an extremely long time. Twelve volt fluorescent units are available, but they are comparatively expensive, since each unit contains a power source similar to the Heathkit convertor. By using the standard household fixtures, you have the added advantage of a wide variety of tubes to choose from and almost universal availability if you should ever happen to have to replace a tube.

With this arrangement it is extremely simple to operate these fluorescent fixtures on dockside current when it is at hand. No transformer is needed nor any double set of wiring. Just a single switch to shift from convertor to dockside.

A SIMPLE WAY OF COMPENSATING
YOUR COMPASS

If your steering compass shows any large errors (in excess of 6° or 7°), it is worth compensating it rather than leaving the error in and allowing for it by the use of a deviation chart. It should be possible, especially in a sailing boat, to reduce the deviation to an almost negligible amount by a relatively simple procedure. This assumes that the compass is mounted as high as possible above the engine, and that no electric wires or apparatus containing steel or iron are located near it.

Some yacht compasses have built-in compensators, in which case you will not have to use separate magnets. Just follow the steps to be described here, but turn the adjusting screws to obtain the desired corrections instead of moving the magnets as I shall describe.

In the discussion to follow, I shall assume that your compass does *not* contain built-in compensators. The first step, therefore, is to obtain a pair of compensating magnets from your chandler. They are small rectangular bar magnets with a tack hole in either end. Have a few copper tacks at hand for the job, along with some adhesive tape and a hammer. Take along a couple of brightly colored deck cushions of the type approved for flotation.

Decide where you wish to mount the magnets. One must go either directly ahead of the compass or directly aft from it. The other must be located directly athwartships from the compass, either to port or starboard. Their distance from the compass remains to be determined, but will probably be within a couple of feet. Try to select positions where the magnets can be left permanently, so this will probably be the underside of the coach roof if the compass is mounted on the dog-house, or the underside of a cockpit bench if the compass is mounted in the bridge deck. Prepare some short pieces of adhesive tape to hold the magnets in position during the compensating procedure.

Pick a calm day when the water is undisturbed, and take along a friend who is a good helmsman. It is best to do the actual adjustments under power, as you can select the exact course you wish to steer. Have your helmsman put the boat on a northerly course and drop one of the cushions overboard as a marker. Hold an absolutely straight course for a few hundred yards, and make a note of this exact heading. Let us say the compass reads 4°. Now drop a second cushion overboard and continue on course for another few hundred yards. Have the helmsman come about and bring the two cushions directly into line dead ahead, as represented in Figure 37. When he has them exactly in range, have him hold a steady course while you make a note of the compass heading. Let us say that this turns out to be 172°. Incidentally, for the time being, keep the compensating magnets stowed well away from the compass.

If the compass were perfectly compensated, this second heading would be the exact reciprocal of the original course, or 184°. Of course, if it were perfectly compensated, you wouldn't be fooling around out here getting your cushions wet, would you? Subtract the 4° from the 172°, and you get a difference of 168°, rather than the

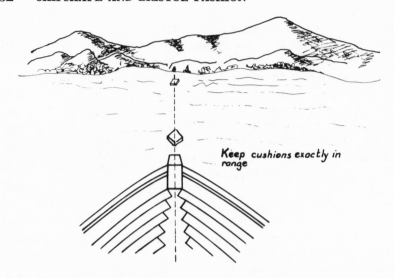

Keep cushions exactly in range

Fig. 37—Cushions in range dead ahead.

180° difference that should exist. So we have a total of 12° (180° − 168°) error in the two legs of the run, and now we want to try to get rid of it. Have the helmsman go on past the first cushion for some distance while you get ready to do your compensating. Several hundred yards beyond the first cushion, have him turn around and get the two cushions lined up again.

Now, while the cushions are held in line, place one of the magnets directly ahead (or abaft) the compass with the magnet itself oriented athwartships. Move it toward the compass keeping it on the fore and aft line as shown in Figure 38. Don't change the magnet's orientation; just move it fore and aft and see what effect it has on the compass. You want to *subtract* half of the 12° error from the compass reading. Half of 12° is 6°, and this subtracted from the original course reading of 4° gives 358° for the heading you want to establish on the compass. If moving the magnet in toward the compass produces a change in the wrong direction, turn the magnet end for end. Keep moving the magnet along the fore and aft line until the compass reads 358°. At this point, stick the magnet down securely with the adhesive tape.

Have your helmsman swing out around the second cushion (unless you want a propellor full of kapok), go on past for some distance, and then come about and line up the cushions for another southerly run.

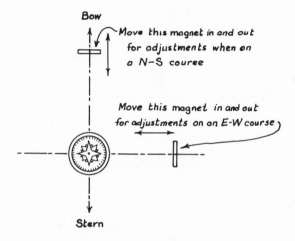

Bow

Move this magnet in and out
for adjustments when on
a N-S course

Move this magnet in and out
for adjustments on an E-W course

Stern

Fig. 38—Adjustment of compensating magnets.

This time, as he keeps the cushions exactly in range, the compass should read the exact reciprocal of 358°, or 178°. If it doesn't, make another pass and adjust out half of the difference. You should now be right on the button.

Now pick up the cushions, and repeat the entire procedure starting on an easterly heading. Let us say that your first course is 87°, and that your compass, as you come back on the first reciprocal leg, reads 273°. It should read 267°, shouldn't it? Instead there is a 186° difference between the courses run, so we have an error of 6° to get rid of, and we shall do this by adjusting out half of it, or 3°, on our next run.

Run down the easterly course again, this time positioning the second magnet on the athwartships line (reversing it if necessary) to make the compass read exactly 90°, or 3° more than it did the first time. Pass the second cushion, and come back again along the range of the two cushions. This time your compass should read exactly 270°. If it doesn't, make another run and adjust out half of the remaining error.

Now, let us formalize this so we may have some definite rules for the procedure. Let D_z = the difference between the first heading and the second or return heading. Just subtract the smaller from the larger. The amount of correction to introduce by positioning the magnet will always be:

$$\text{Correction} = \frac{D_z \sim 180°}{2}$$

The symbol $\sim$ denotes the simple arithmetic difference between D_z and 180°. Forget about the sign and just subtract the smaller from the larger. Half of this difference is the *amount* of compensation to introduce with the magnet.

The *direction* of this correction is most easily determined by drawing a simple diagram, as shown in Figure 39. Do this on a piece of tracing paper taped over a compass rose on one of your charts. For example, in our first northerly run the compass read 4°. Draw a line

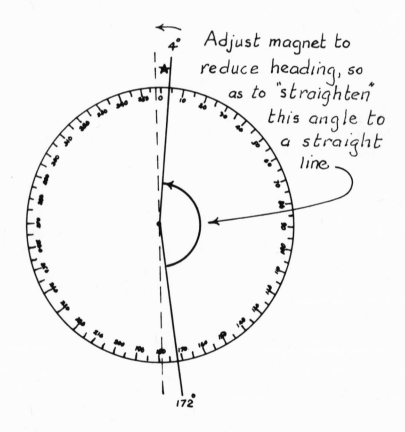

Adjust magnet to reduce heading, so as to "straighten" this angle to a straight line.

Fig. 39—Diagram to determine direction of necessary compensation.

from the center of the rose through 4°. The return course was 172°, so draw this in next and you should have something looking like Figure 39.

Notice that the two courses form a slight angle to each other. Our goal is to "straighten" this out by applying half the error as a correction to each end of the bent line. You can easily see that the upper half of the line must be "bent" to the left, or counterclockwise, so you will adjust the magnet to reduce the compass heading on your next northerly run.

All this assumes that your compass reads from 0° to 360° as most modern yacht compasses do. If you have a different type of card, the same reasoning will apply. Adjust the magnet so as to deflect the compass in the direction which will "straighten out" this plotted line.

When your adjustment is complete, tack the magnets in place and protect them with a couple of coats of paint. If you wish to be really accurate, swing your compass now, as described on page 98. Most of the error should have disappeared, but there may be a little residual error on some headings, in which case you should prepare a deviation chart. It is also a good idea to check for deviation arising from your engine's electrical system. Hold a steady course under power, and then turn the engine off and see if the compass reading changes noticeably. If having the engine running introduces any marked change you will have to prepare two deviation charts—one for power and one for sail.

Your compass should now be good for several years unless you install a new engine, change the rigging, or otherwise alter the magnetic environment of the compass. Just to be safe, however, take advantage of any opportunities you have while cruising to check the compass from landmarks in range, sun bearings, etc.

ARE YOUR INSTRUMENTS ACCURATE?

All too often we *assume* that an instrument is accurate without bothering to find out. Sometimes this can lead to very annoying and costly errors. Not long ago I bought a combination square of a very well-known brand and began using it in my shop. Some time later I began to realize that the joints in the cabinet work I was doing were not fitting as well as I might wish. I checked the square (which I *should* have done when I bought it) and found that it was nearly two degrees out of square. I spent the better part of an afternoon reworking the joint in the square, and now I'm much less unhappy with my cabinet work. The fact remains, however, that I turned out some pretty bad joints and then spent several hours virtually remaking a supposedly precision tool.

Now, just what do I mean when I ask, "Are your instruments accurate?" Every tool, whether it be a simple straightedge, a drafting triangle, a micrometer, or a radio direction finder is bought to do a particular job or range of jobs. I simply mean, then, "Is the instrument accurate enough to do the job for which you wish to use it?" I want my micrometers, for example, to be as accurate as I can get and keep them. I want my drafting instruments to be no more in error than the width of the thinnest line I am able to draw. On the other hand, I know I can't read a magnetic compass at sea closer than one degree at best, so I'll settle for any error that doesn't exceed that amount.

Sometimes, as in the case of the combination square, the error has to be removed to make the instrument usable. In other instances, such as a radio direction finder, it is enough if we know what the error is and are able to allow for it in our calculations and plotting. Keep in mind, then, that when I use the word *calibrate,* I am referrring only to the *determination* of the error, and I shall use the terms *adjust* or *compensate* when I am talking about *removing* the error.

Parts of this discussion will have to do with tests to use in buying a new instrument, and if the instrument doesn't pass the test you should lay it aside and try another. These same tests can be used and should be used on instruments you already have. I'll try, wherever I can, to suggest practical ways in which you can adjust your inaccurate instruments, rather than buying new ones.

A good quality instrument from a well-known manufacturer is less likely to be in error than is a cheap one, but this should not be taken for granted. I recently bought some new drafting triangles with a well-known trademark. I tried five before I found a pair that were satisfactory, and two of them were in error more than a degree in the right angle. On the other hand, I have a pair of parallel rules which I bought for almost nothing in a war surplus store, and they are as accurate as any I have ever seen. It is true that I checked out several pairs and selected the best. Most instrument dealers will not resent your testing an instrument before buying it. If they do, take your business elsewhere.

You pay good money for precision in instruments, and you should expect to get it.

CHARTING AND DRAFTING INSTRUMENTS

Straightedges. The simpler the instrument, the more likely one is to assume that it is all right. A straightedge is supposed to be straight, but *is* it? There is a simple way of finding out, and this applies to any edge of any instrument you may wish to use for ruling a straight line.

Draw a line along the edge (Figure 40) using a sharp hard pencil in-

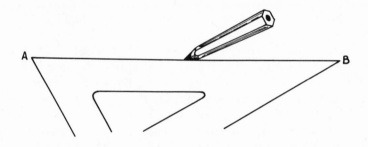

Fig. 40—Line drawn close against straightedge.

clined away from the edge so the pencil point is close up against the straightedge. Then, as shown in Figure 41, turn the straightedge over (*don't* turn it end for end), and check the edge against the line you have just drawn. If the edge is really straight, it should lie perfectly along the line throughout its entire length. If there are sections where the edge stands out away from the line, this means there are hollows in the straightedge where this occurs, and you should lay it aside and try another. The edge of the triangle shown in Figure 41 is definitely concave and should be rejected.

Adjusting errors in a straightedge is a very difficult procedure, especially if the instrument is very long. You will, of course, have to remove some of the material between the hollows you have just detected. As you do this, you must be very careful not to introduce new errors, nor to produce a slightly convex edge, since one generally tends to remove more material from the end portions than from the center. Mark the areas to be dressed down, then carefully reduce them with

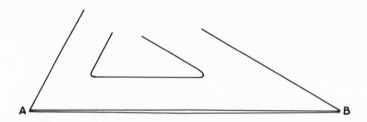

Fig. 41—Straightedge (triangle) inverted and tested against drawn line. Note hollow in middle portion—edge is concave.

a sharp, finely cut mill file held so that its entire length is kept in contact with the straightedge.

After taking just a few strokes over the high areas, draw a new line with the straightedge, invert it, check it against this new line, and remark the high spots. This may have to be done many times before you are finally satisfied with the result. Shorter edges, such as the edge of a plastic triangle or a metal try square can be more easily straightened, but the procedure is the same, at least in principle.

For these shorter edges, obtain a sheet of plate glass somewhat longer than the edge to be worked on, and lay it on a flat surface. Get two sheets of abrasive paper. For metal or plastic I like to use an aluminum oxide paper of about 220 grit to remove the irregularities and about 600 grit to smooth out the scratches. Lay the paper on the glass, abrasive side up, and very carefully and slowly rub the straightedge against it. Take care to keep the entire length of the straightedge on the paper at all times, and hold the body of the straightedge perpendicular to the paper surface. Check the edge frequently as you adjust it.

Triangles. A pair of drafting triangles are useful plotting instruments, as well as being invaluable for making sketches and plans for alterations you wish to make aboard your yacht. To be of use, however, they should really possess the angles they are supposed to have. Test them first to make sure all edges are straight, then test the various angles as follows:

1. *To test the 90° angle,* many salesmen, and draftsmen too, I am afraid, will place two triangles back to back against a T-square, as shown in Figure 42, and see if the vertical edges are perfectly in con-

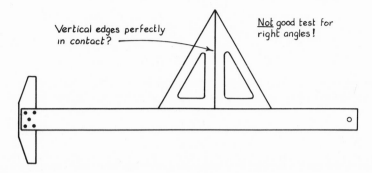

Fig. 42—A *common but* inadequate *test for right angles.*

tact. This is *not* a good test. All it tells you is whether the two angles add up to 180°. If so, this *may* mean that they are both 90° angles, but it can just as well mean that one of them is 91° and the other 89°, or any similar combination. If the edges do *not* meet perfectly, you still do not know which, if either, of the two is accurate.

A much better test is to place the triangle against a T-square, as shown in Figure 43, and carefully draw a line along the vertical edge. Keeping the T-square in place, reverse the triangle as shown in Figure 44 and check the vertical edge against the line you have drawn. If it lines up perfectly, the angle is exactly 90°. Before doing this, test the T-square to make sure its edge is straight, since this is an assumption on

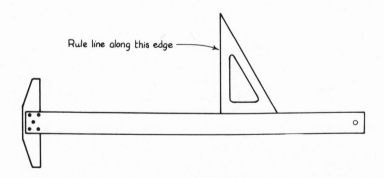

Fig. 43—*Draw line along vertical edge, using a T-square that has been tested for straightness.*

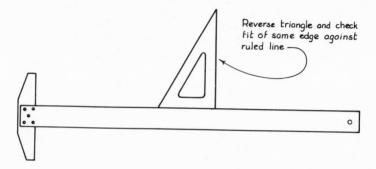

Fig. 44—Reverse triangle and test vertical edge against drawn line.

which this test is based. When you find a triangle that passes this test, you can use it as shown in Figure 42 to check other right angles.

2. *To test the 30° angle,* place the triangle on a fresh sheet of paper and carefully draw lines along the two sides as shown in Figure 45.

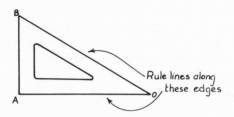

Fig. 45—Rule lines along two sides of 30° angle.

Shift the triangle, lining it up exactly with line OB and draw line OC as shown in Figure 46. In doing this you are adding the angle to itself. Shift it again so that it exactly lines up with the last line drawn and draw line OD, as shown in Figure 47. Now test angle AOD with the 90° angle *you have just tested.* It should agree exactly. If it doesn't, either the 30° angle is inaccurate or you have made a slight drafting error. Check it again and if it is still off, try another triangle.

3. *To test the 60° angle,* is superfluous, since it must be correct if the 90° and 30° angles are accurate.

4. *To test the 45° angle,* repeat the procedure shown in Figures 45 and 46, but draw only two angles this time. In doing so, be sure you

*Fig. 46—Shift triangle and rule line OC,
thus doubling first angle drawn in Figure 45.*

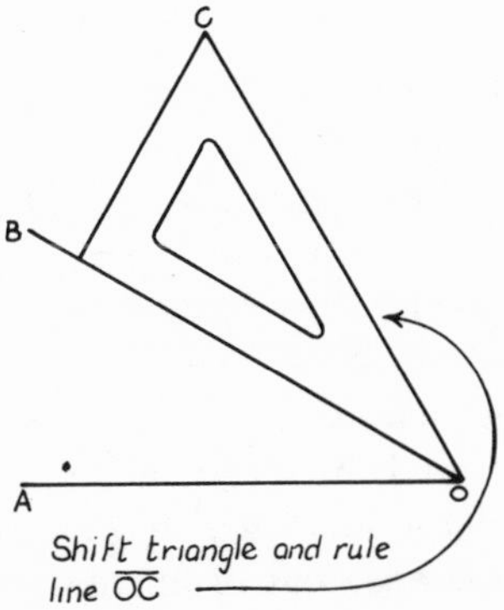

Shift triangle and rule
line $\overline{OC}$

use the *same* corner of the plastic triangle to draw *both* these angles.
Test the sum of these two angles with an already tested right angle. If
the fit is perfect, the triangle is accurate and the other 45° angle need
not be tested if you have checked the right angle.

To *adjust an inaccurate triangle,* use the glass plate and abrasive
paper already described, but be prepared for a difficult job. To alter the
angle, you must sand down one end of the edge more than the other.
In doing this you are very likely to produce a convex edge, so you
must continue to check the edge for straightness as well as checking
the size of the angle as you work. Take it slowly and it can be done.

Parallel rules. Provide yourself with a sheet of *good quality* engineer's
graph paper large enough so the entire length of the parallel rule may

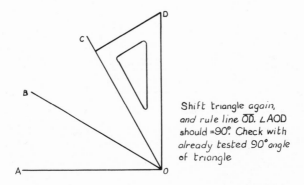

Shift triangle again,
and rule line $\overline{OD}$. ∠AOD
should =90°. Check with
already tested 90°angle
of triangle

Fig. 47—Shift triangle once more and rule line OD.

be placed on it. Get paper made by a reputable firm such as Post or Dietzgen or Keuffel and Esser, and get it ruled in millimeter squares if possible.

First test the edges of the parallel rules to see if they are straight. If they are, check the joints in the rule next. To do this, lay the rule on the graph paper and line up an edge with one of the lines on the paper. Now, press down hard on the other half of the rule to hold it in place and wiggle the loose or unsupported half with your other hand. Watch the edge's alignment with the lines on the paper as you do this. If the joints are in good condition, you should hardly be able to twist the edge out of alignment without also moving the half you are holding. If there is an appreciable looseness, put the rule back and try another. It is difficult to tighten the joints in most parallel rules.

Next test the parallelism of the outside edges of the rule when it is closed. Place it on the graph paper as shown in Figure 48, with its lower edge exactly along one of the lines on the paper. Now check the upper edge of the rule. It may not lie exactly on one of the ruled lines, but it should be exactly parallel to them. With finely ruled paper, any significant error in this regard will be readily detected by your eye.

If the rule passes this test, continue to hold the bottom section in line with the graph paper, and open the rule fully as shown in Figure 49. The upper edge should still be exactly parallel to the horizontal lines on the paper. If it passes this test, ask to use a large size Mercator chart—any such chart will do, but the bigger the better. Carefully align

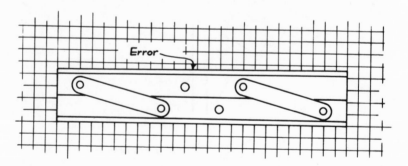

Fig. 48—Upper and lower edges are not parallel.

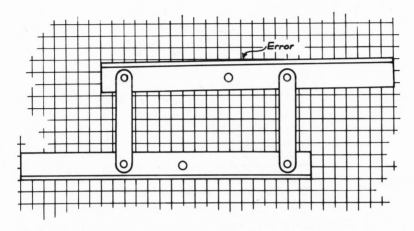

Fig. 49—Rule which will step out of parallel.

the parallel rule with a meridian near one edge of the chart. Very carefully step the rule across the entire chart until you reach the last meridian near the opposite edge. It should still be parallel to the edge of the rule. If not, try it again to make certain you did not allow it to slip while stepping it across the chart. If it still fails to check out, put it aside. With care, one can adjust slight errors in a triangle, but a parallel rule which steps out of parallel is almost impossible to adjust. If you already own it, throw it away.

Protractors made by reputable manufacturers are usually very accurately divided. This can be spot-checked, however. Lay the protractor on a sheet of paper, and mark the position of the bottom edge and the center hole. Now carefully mark on the paper several different angles and label them as shown in Figure 50. Invert the protractor and reposition its bottom edge and center hole on your marks. Now, with the protractor upside down, note the readings opposite the labelled marks you made on the paper. You will, of course, be reading through the back of the protractor and all the readings will be backward. The angles should now measure the same difference from 90°, but in the opposite direction. For example, as shown in Figure 51, the mark labelled "60°" should now lie exactly opposite 120° (60° is thirty degrees *less* than 90°, and 120° is thirty degrees *more* than 90°). Simi-

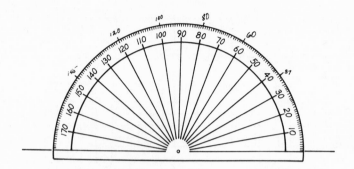

Fig. 50—Mark several angles and label them.

larly, the "145°" mark should now line up with 35° on the protractor, etc. Except in very cheap protractors, you will not be likely to find significant errors in these scales.

The most common error, and it can be a serious one, is in the location of the center hole. This may be significantly off center. It can be checked by laying the protractor over a straightedge, lining it up so that the straightedge passes exactly through the 0° and 180° marks, and checking to see if the center mark or hole also lies exactly on the straightedge. It should also be directly under the vertical line running to the 90° mark. The scales are stamped or printed on and are usually quite accurate, but the holes are often punched or drilled in a subsequent operation, and may be badly out of position.

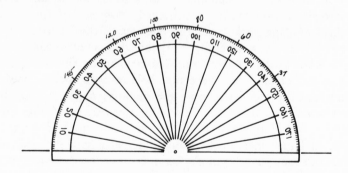

Fig. 51—Invert protractor and check marked angles.

Aircraft-type course plotters are usually quite accurate, but testing them takes very little time, so why take a chance? First test the edges to see if they are straight. If they are, test with graph paper to see if the upper and lower edges are parallel. At the same time check the horizontal lines usually engraved on the "ruler" portion of the plotter to make sure they are parallel to the upper and lower edges.

Now check to make sure that the upper edge of the "ruler" portion is in line with the center hole and the 0° and 180° marks. This is easily done by laying the plotter on top of a straightedge, preferably opaque or colored so it can be seen easily through the plotter. Press down, as shown in Figure 52 enough to bend the "arms" of the plotter

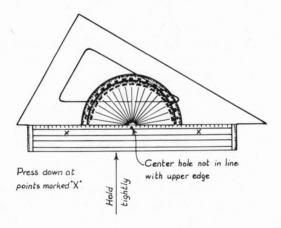

Fig. 52—*Checking position of center hole in aircraft-type plotter. Hole shown is too low.*

down a bit, then shove it up tight against the straight edge. Holding it in this position, look straight down on it, and see if the straightedge passes exactly through the center hole and the two end marks on the protractor scale.

Course plotters with swiveling arms are best bought with a square protractor card (as shown in Figure 53), rather than a round one. The square card, carrying a rectangular grid, makes it possible to line up any edge of the card, or any line of the grid with a meridian or parallel on

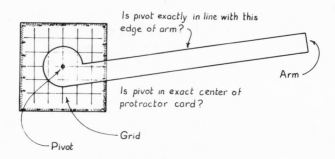

Fig. 53—Recommended card shape for this type of plotter. Rectangular grid can be lined up with meridian or parallel on Mercator chart.

the chart. With the circular type, one has to look down through the small hole in the center of the pivot to see the meridian and this is not always easy to do without the best of lighting. Check this instrument as I have described for the aircraft plotter, to make certain that the pointer edge of the arm is exactly aligned with the pivot hole. Then check to see that the pivot is placed exactly *in the center of the card.* I have seen several of these that were beautifully made, but which had been incorrectly assembled with the pivot nearly an eighth of an inch from the center of the card.

If you are assessing one of these, with the intention of buying it, make certain that the hollow rivet or pivot is made of a non-corrosive metal such as stainless steel or Monel. A steel rivet will rust in no time, and a brass one turns a vile green which rubs off on the charts.

Chart dividers should be judged in terms of their rigidity, smoothness of the joint action, and their material. They should have little or no flexibility in their legs, and you can test this by squeezing their points together gently, using a slight pressure so as not to move the joint. You should see no appreciable movement of the points. If there is much "spring" of this sort, you will find it is difficult to use them on a chart because of the backlash.

The heavy marine type shown in Figure 54 are very good. I like the one-hand type shown in Figure 55 best, since they can really be used with one hand, and this is an advantage at times. The joints should be smooth throughout the limits of their movement. They should be adjustable for tension, and I like the adjustment shown in

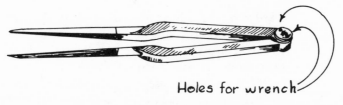

Holes for wrench

Fig. 54—Chart dividers. Note that a special two-pronged wrench is required for adjusting tension of joint.

Figure 55. It is a slot which permits you to use the edge of a coin rather than the special double-pointed wrench needed for the type shown in Figure 54.

The most beautifully made dividers in the world will look and work like a piece of junk in a few weeks at sea, if they are not made from corrosion resistant materials. The types shown in Figure 55 usually have a brass or bronze joint section, but the legs are often carbon steel which rusts badly in salt air. They *can* be had with stainless legs, and these should be insisted upon. If you are in doubt about the material, ask to borrow a small magnetic compass. It may show some activity as you move it past a stainless leg, but it will go wild when you bring it near a carbon steel leg.

Pencil compasses should also be made of stainless steel throughout, and this should be carefully checked by the use of a small magnetic compass. I have seen several stainless steel compasses that quickly fell apart because some of the tiny screws and nuts holding the pencil leg and the tensioning mechanism in the joint were carbon steel. Again,

Slot for coin

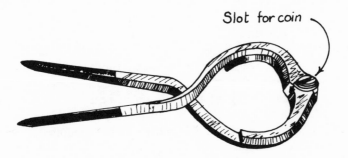

Fig. 55—One-hand chart dividers. Joint can be tightened with edge of coin.

this can be checked with a magnetic compass. The needle point in the center leg of the compass is also likely to be of carbon steel unless you insist otherwise. The compass should have an extension leg, since this allows you to draw an arc of nearly ten inch radius. It is a very inexpensive addition, and I find that I use it often enough to justify it.

Add a few soft pencils and a good eraser and your plotting outfit is now complete. Moreover, you know that it is *accurate*, and with this accuracy established you can go on to check your compass, radio direction finder, echo sounder, and log.

NAVIGATING INSTRUMENTS

Magnetic compasses are available in a wide variety of models and there are many good ones among those available. I am so impressed with the superiority of the Sestrel, however, that I'll make a point of explaining why. First of all, it can be read from the top or from the side, and this means that it can be mounted quite high. I have mine on top of the doghouse in the exact centerline of the yacht. This removes it as far as possible from the engine and iron keel, and also gives a 360° clear field of vision for use as a bearing compass. With the sighting vane that comes with it, this is an excellent bearing compass. It is much better damped than any hand bearing compass I have ever used, and, being fixed in position, its deviation never varies in use. I have found changes of deviation amounting to four or five degrees when moving a hand bearing compass from one side of the cockpit to the other. The Sestrel-Moore compass is manufactured by Henry Browne & Son, Ltd., and is distributed in America by the Kenyon Instrument Company of Guilford, Connecticut.

Regardless of your choice of compass, try to mount it in such a way that you can take your bearings with it, rather than having to rely on a hand bearing compass or pelorus which just complicates your charting and introduces another possible source of plotting error. It is also wise to locate the steering compass where the sun falls on it. This enables you to swing the compass using the sun's azimuth as a reference, and you can do this at any location in harbor or at sea. I'll describe this method first, since it is the most universally applicable.

The first method is also more complicated. It requires a Nautical Almanac or Air Almanac, azimuth tables such as H.O.214, and some experience in their use. This can easily be done by any offshore yachtsman who can plot a position line from a sun sight.

If you have not done any celestial navigation, the necessary background for the use of this method can be had by studying Mixter's *Primer of Navigation.** Until you feel reasonably sure of your ability to handle sun sights and their reduction, use the second method of swinging your compass. It depends only upon a knowledge of charting and piloting.

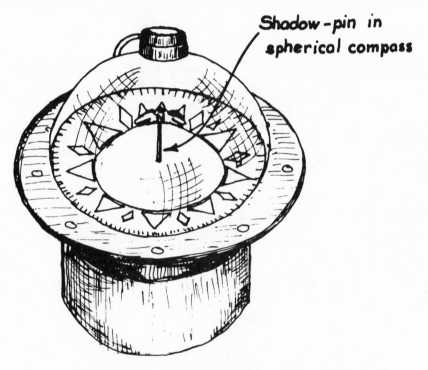

Shadow-pin in spherical compass

Fig. 56a—Spherical-type yacht compass with self-contained shadow pin.

1. First Method (Sun's azimuth): Make sure your compass has a shadow pin of some sort. The spherical type compasses, such as that shown in Figure 56a have a small vertical pin in the center for this purpose. The Sestrel (Figure 56b) has a brass pin that fits into the boss which takes the sighting vane. If you have a flat top compass,

* George W. Mixter, *Primer of Navigation*, edited by Donald McClench (5th ed., Princeton, N.J.: D. Van Nostrand Company, Inc., 1967).

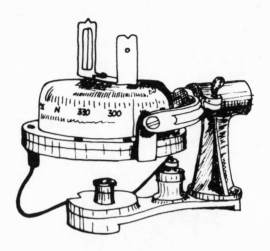

Fig. 56b—Sestrel "Moore" Compass.

such as that shown in Figure 57, you can easily make a plastic disk which supports a vertical brass or Monel wire. Make sure the wire is perpendicular to the disk and that it is non-magnetic. Cut the disk so it will just fit inside the bezel which holds the glass face in the compass and will turn freely in this recess. Scribe a line across this disk passing through the pinhole at one end and running through

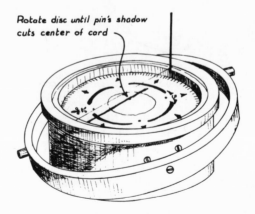

Fig. 57—"Flat top" compass.

the *exact center* of the disk. If you add a second pin at the other end of the line, this disk will work very well for an azimuth ring, and you can use it to take bearings as well as to swing the compass. (See Figure 58.)

Fig. 58—Sighting disk (azimuth ring) for flat top compass.

Clear plostic disc with scribed center line ond shadow pins. Second pin is used as o sight when disc is used for azimuth circle

Now make up a chart such as shown in Figure 59, or clip a piece of tracing paper over the one in this book and use it for your entries. Choose a day when the sky is clear and when there is little or no wind, if you want to make it as easy as possible. Sail out to an anchorage where you are well away from steel bridges, etc., and on the way get a time signal and set your watch accurately to GMT. Plan your day so that you can start swinging your compass early in the morning. You will want the sun high enough to cast a shadow across the face of your compass, but no higher. The higher the sun the faster its azimuth changes, and the greater the errors which will result from slight inaccuracies in timing. Under *no* circumstances attempt to use this method when the sun's altitude is greater than 50°. As this procedure cannot be hurried, the advantages of an early start are obvious.

Drop your anchor and put your dinghy over the side. Set up the shadow pin in your compass, and have a crew member get in the dinghy and tow the stern of your yacht around so the wind is dead aft. If he then lets her swing, the yacht should turn slowly through 180° until it is heading into the wind. As it does this, make entries in your chart for each 20° change in heading. I like to fill in the heading column beforehand, 0°, 20°, 40°, and so on. It eliminates one more

G.M.T.		Comp. Heading	C. Bearing of Shadow	C. Bearing of Sun	True Az. of Sun	Mag. E- Var. W+	Mag. Az. of Sun	Dev. E. W.	

Compass Deviation From Sun's Azimuth

Fig. 59—Tabulating form for swinging a compass using the sun's azimuth. Tape a piece of tracing paper over this to record your data.

entry to make at the time. When you finish this, you should have 18 entries of time and *back* azimuth. If you are doubtful about any, or have missed one or two, swing her once more until you are satisfied with the lot. The calculations can be done when you get home, if you can wait that long.

Establish your position as closely as possible and record the *latitude* and *longitude*. The computations are most easily accomplished with the Air Almanac and H.O. 214. From the Air Almanac, for the day of the observations, take out G.H.A. sun and declination sun. The declination should not change appreciably during the period of your observation, but take out G.H.A. for *every ten minutes* over the period which your entries cover. This can be done by inspection from the Air Almanac with no interpolation at all.

Convert G.H.A. to L.H.A. by subtracting your longitude if it is West, or adding it if it is East, and reduce L.H.A. to meridian angle (t). This is most easily done as described by Mixter: "Add East Longitude to G.H.A. If sum exceeds 360°, subtract 360°. Subtract West Longitude from G.H.A., if necessary having added 360° to G.H.A. to permit subtraction. If either result be less than 180°, it is the value of t (W). If it exceeds 180°, subtract it from 360° to find the value of t (E)."

With the various values for t, representing ten minute intervals, enter the tables in H.O.214 for the declination and latitude nearest those actually pertaining, and take out the corresponding azimuths. There is no need to correct for *latitude difference*, since the correction, if the altitude is less than 50° would be less than half a degree in most cases, and this is a finer measurement than your compass readings.

Make a graph, plotting G.M.T. against azimuth, as shown in Figure 60. Connect your plotted points with a smooth fair curve, and you can interpolate the azimuth for any of the intervening times.

From these interpolations, fill in the *true azimuth* column on the form, making an entry for each of the recorded times. Obtain the local magnetic variation, corrected to the current year, and apply it to these azimuths to give you the *magnetic azimuths*. Enter these in the appropriate column on the form.

The differences between the magnetic azimuth and the compass bearing of the sun will give the deviation for each of the 20° entries.

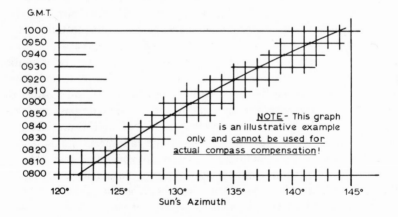

Fig. 60—Example of graph of sun's azimuth plotted against time over two hour period. Intermediate values can be quite accurately interpolated.

Calculate these deviations and enter them in the deviation column. Now you can either make a deviation curve, or simply list these in tabular form and post them by your chart table.

This method, while more demanding than the one to be described next, is worth learning. Each time you reduce a sun sight at sea, in order to plot a position line, you obtain the sun's azimuth. If you take a compass bearing of the sun at the same time the sight is taken, you can check your compass with each sight reduction. The fact that this method can be done equally well off shore makes it well worth knowing.

2. Second Method (Swinging the compass): To swing a magnetic compass by bearings on an object on shore is simpler and does not require the use of any celestial tables or calculations. It does require accurate plotting instruments, and you should now have these. It can be done on a cloudy day if there is good visibility, but it should be done in calm water and a light wind.

Anchor in a spot where you have a good view of an accurately definable landmark such as a tower, sharp mountain peak, road junction, etc., and be sure that this landmark is clearly and unequivocally located on your chart. Anchor with a short scope to minimize your swinging circle—just enough chain to be sure you'll not drag the anchor.

Locate your exact position by ranges or by horizontal sextant angles between easily identified landmarks on shore. Use at least four such landmarks to give you a check on the accuracy of your plotted position. You should have it pinpointed to within two hundred yards.

From this position, lay off the bearing to the tower or mountain peak you plan to use, and this landmark should be at least three or four miles away. Take the true bearing from the chart and convert this to magnetic. Now put the sighting vane on your compass and have someone tow the yacht around just as described in the preceding discussion. At every 20° take a bearing of the landmark and note these bearings and the corresponding headings on your note pad. The differences between these compass bearings and the magnetic azimuth of the landmark, as taken from the chart, will be the deviations. These can be tabulated as you see fit and posted for your reference.

Around your club or local sailing grounds, there will be a number of ranges you can identify. Buoys marking the entrance channel, two headlands in range, water towers, etc. Prepare a list of these ranges and the exact bearing which each represents, taking this off your chart of the area. With this list at hand, you can check your compass on several headings each time you enter and leave your berth or anchorage, and this is a fine habit to get into.

A few years ago, while sailing at night, I saw a solid wall of fog approaching me. I quickly swung the yacht around, lined it up on the North Star which was clearly visible, and glanced at the compass. It showed not the 2° deviation I expected but 17°. Then the fog hit and I could barely see the bow from the cockpit. We were in a crowded area with lots of traffic, and it was as close to our destination as it would have been to turn back. I dashed below and noticed a new cabin lamp which I had mounted a couple of days previously on the opposite side of the bulkhead on which the compass was mounted. I ripped the lamp off the bulkhead and stowed it forward. As I did so, my helmsman reported a 15° swing in the compass reading. We made seven miles that night on fathometer and compass, and couldn't see the harbor until we were inside it, but it taught me a lesson about compass errors. You just can't afford *not* to check your compass when ever you have a good chance. The fact that it checked out all right two days ago doesn't mean a thing, if someone has set a transistor radio or an exposure meter near it this morning.

If your deviation chart shows compass error in excess of 6° or 7°, you should compensate your compass. This will remove most of the error present. A simple method of compass compensation has been described on page 80.

Radio direction finders require calibrating too, and a failure to do this often leads to their being judged unreliable when they could really be of great value. I have seen very few yachts carrying deviation charts for their RDF, although nearly all of them have one for the magnetic compass. This is difficult to understand, since the RDF is an expensive piece of equipment, and will perform very reliably if given a chance. It may be possible, in a power boat, simply to install one and then go ahead and use it with a reasonable degree of success, but such is seldom if ever the case in a sailboat.

The maze of standing rigging does some strange things to the radio waves, and this cannot be corrected as can the magnetic disturbances which affect the compass. This effect is actually made use of in television and FM antennas, where only one rod of the array acts as the antenna proper, and the rest serve to reflect or focus the electromagnetic energy onto the active element. The stays and shrouds of the standing rigging act in much the same way, and serve to refract and distort the radio waves.

Since this cannot be compensated out, and since sailboat rigs are such individual affairs, one can only plot and allow for the effects of the rigging. One consolation is that this does not vary with latitude nor with geographic location, so that once the job is done it should not need to be repeated unless the rig is altered.

If you have a friend or crew member who is familiar enough with your RDF to operate it reliably, you can calibrate it at the same time you swing your magnetic compass. Have him continue to maintain a null or minimum signal setting on the RDF. Call out each 20° heading as the yacht swings through it, and have him note this along with his radio bearing of the beacon being used for the calibration. This beacon, incidentally, should be more than five and less than fifty miles away, and should lie across open water from you without any appreciable amount of intervening land. When you have finished swinging the ship, he should have for you a table of 18 compass headings with a radio bearing of the beacon opposite each.

For the reduction of this data to a form from which a deviation chart can be made, use the data form shown in Figure 61. You can lay a piece of tracing paper over it, and do your calculations, using a separate piece of tracing paper for each of the 18 headings for which you have data. For this procedure, I shall assume that your RDF uses a loop antenna which gives you a reading *relative to the heading of the yacht*. If you use one of the directional antennas that are combined with a plotting instrument, this will also enable you to use the table in Figure 61, since you will still have a table of relative radio bearings from which to work. On the other hand, if your RDF antenna is the type that incorporates its own magnetic compass, you will have to convert the readings to relative bearings before beginning the calculations. With this type of instrument, do not overlook the fact that its own magnetic compass should be checked for deviation, since its deviation may be quite different from that of the steering compass.

Begin your calculations by entering one of the 18 compass headings in the top space of the form. In the next space below, enter the compass deviation for this heading (you have just determined this) and label it E or W as the case may be. Subtract this deviation if it is

		E or W
Compass Heading		
Compass Deviation (E or W) (Add if E, Subtract if W)		
Magnetic Heading		
Magnetic Variation (E or W) (Add if E, Subtract if W)		
True Heading		
RDF Bearing (Relative) (Add)		
Azimuth $_{RDF}$	360°	
Azimuth $_{Chart}$ (Take Diff ∼)		
RDF Deviation Name W if Az $_{RDF}$ is larger Name E if Az $_{Chart}$ is larger		

Fig. 61—Tabulating form for RDF calibration.

W, or add it if it is E and enter the result as the *magnetic heading* on the next line. Below this, enter the current *magnetic variation* for your location, taken from a chart of the area, and label this E or W. Add, if it is E, or subtract, if it is W, to obtain the *true heading* which is to be entered on the next line.

Enter the tabulated RDF bearing (a relative bearing) for this heading in the next space, and add this to the *true heading*. This will give you the RDF azimuth of the radio beacon. If the sum thus obtained is greater than 360°, subtract 360° from it and enter the remainder as the RDF azimuth.

Take the true azimuth of the radio beacon, relative to your anchored position, off the chart and enter it in the next line of the form. This value will be the same for all 18 of the computations. Now, the difference between this true azimuth taken from the chart and the RDF azimuth will be the RDF deviation for this relative bearing. Enter it on the bottom line. If the RDF azimuth was the larger of the two, name this deviation W. If the azimuth taken from the chart was larger, name the deviation E. Be careful on a northerly heading, if one of the azimuths lies west of north and the other lies east of north. In this instance, add 360° to the azimuth which lies east of north and then follow the rule given above.

Since the disturbance in the RDF readings comes from the effect of the yacht's rigging, your deviation chart must be set up to show deviations plotted against *relative bearings* rather than against compass headings as for the magnetic compass. You have this data on the forms, so put it in chart form and post it by the RDF.

The combination RDF antennas and hand bearing compasses are intended to free one from the need to consider relative bearings, and supposedly allow you to read the radio bearing (magnetic) directly off the instrument. The fallacy in this is that one has to compute backwards to *obtain* a relative bearing in order to allow for the RDF deviation, and this results in one of two choices. Either one ends up doing as much or more calculation than with the conventional loop, or one ignores the RDF deviation which can be very large at times. For this reason, I much prefer the conventional loop in a sailing boat.

There is one means by which much of this work can be avoided. If one sets the RDF antenna directly athwartships, its null point should be directly fore and aft. By adjusting the angle of the loop slightly to allow for deviation, it can be lined up so that the null reading is always obtained when the ship is directly on course for the beacon. If the antenna is clamped permanently in this position, readings can be taken by changing course until the minimum signal is obtained and reading the compass bearing of the beacon directly off the steering compass. There is much to recommend this arrangement. While it may necessitate more sail handling and maneuvering, it vastly simplifies the correcting and plotting of the radio bearings obtained, and it is always set up properly for use in homing on a beacon.

On a boat with a simple rig, your RDF deviation should remain very constant and reliable. On a larger boat it is well to check to see if there is any significant effect from the shifting of the wire topping lift and running backstays as you go from one tack to the other. Pick a marker buoy surrounded by open water and sail downwind toward it with the sheet eased out and the weather runner set up. Have your observer get a radio bearing of a beacon as you pass the buoy. Now sail back upwind from the buoy and repeat the performance with the boom out on the other side and the other runner set up. Get another radio bearing of the same beacon as you pass the buoy and compare the two. If there is any marked difference, you may have to prepare two deviation charts for your RDF, one for a port tack and the other for a starboard tack. This may sound like a lot of work, and it is, but it will result in your being able to use your RDF with confidence in a pea soup fog, and that is what really justifies its existence.

Before you finish checking out the RDF, make sure that the frequency markings on the tuning dial are accurate. You can always identify a beacon by its characteristic signal, but there are times when it is very convenient to be able to use a standard broadcast station for a bearing, and you'll not wish to wait a quarter of an hour for a station identification. When you do use such broadcast stations, remember that you may get a sizable error from "land effect" if the station is any distance inland, and also that the RDF will give you a bearing on the *transmitting antenna*, so be sure you know where this antenna is located.

When you use your RDF, remember a few things always pointed out in the set's operating instructions but often forgotten or neglected by yachtsmen. Bearings taken on stations more than fifty miles away are of questionable accuracy and should be corrected for difference in latitude. Table 1 in Bowditch allows you to do this quickly. Bearings taken on a station that is inland may be in error as the waves tend to be refracted as they pass the coast.

When you are homing on a beacon, *watch yourself*. The beacon will bring you right in on a collision course, and several ships have been lost by failing to consider this. It is a better practice to sail in on a course which keeps the beacon slightly to one side. You may be able to rely on soundings to tell you when you are getting close. If not, remember that the radio bearings (relative) of the beacon will begin to change very rapidly as you come abeam of it, and this will enable you to get a running fix on the beacon and establish your position quite accurately.

Practice using your RDF in daylight when there is good visibility. Errors you make then will not have any catastrophic result, and you will develop skill in handling the instrument and confidence in its results, and this experience will be a very welcome background when you have to use the RDF in less favorable conditions.

Taff-rail logs are surprisingly accurate if well maintained. My Walker log was several years old when I got it and I have put a good many thousand miles on it since then. It still indicates within two per cent of the distance run, except in unusual conditions such as following seas or very slow speeds. It will not continue to do this forever, however, so I check it whenever I have an opportunity. I want to know about it when its accuracy does begin to fall off.

This is easy enough to do if you are sailing in waters that are essentially free from currents. You just find a couple of landmarks on your chart, measure the distance between them, and sail by streaming the log. Buoys make excellent marks for this purpose and are usually very accurately located on charts. Locate a few such measured distances near your anchorage, and you can always check your log on the way out, if there is no current flowing. If you sail in a tidal area, and most of us do, there are two choices open to you. The simplest is to make your calibration at slack water when there is no current flowing. If you do this, *make sure* there is no current flowing by chucking a piece of paper overboard near a buoy and watching for a little while to see if it stays there.

If there is a current running, the easiest solution is to sail from one buoy to the other, noting your log reading between buoys, then come about and sail back again noting the log reading on the return lap. Now be careful in the way in which you compute the results. Let's take an illustrative example.

Suppose that you are sailing over a measured mile at 6 knots, and that there is a 4 knot current setting directly against you. You will make 2 knots over the bottom and will take 30 minutes to sail from buoy to buoy. Now, if you come about and sail back, you will be making good 10 knots over the bottom and will take 6 minutes to sail the return lap. In the first instance, since you sailed at 6 knots through the water for 30 minutes, your log will read 3 miles. On the return leg, still sailing at 6 knots through the water but for only 6 minutes, your log will read 0.6 miles. If you average these two distances, you arrive at the obviously erroneous conclusion that the buoys are 1.8 miles apart, or that your log is hopelessly inaccurate.

The calculations must be made on the basis of *speed* rather than distance. You must accurately time your passage from buoy to buoy. Assume that your log actually reads 2.8 miles on the upstream leg and 0.56 miles on the downstream leg. Two and eight tenths miles in

30 minutes makes your speed through the water 5.6 knots, by the log. You know that you made good 2 knots over the bottom, so you assume a current of 3.6 knots setting against you. On the downstream leg, at 5.6 knots in 6 minutes you would have covered 0.56 miles through the water. You know you covered one mile over the bottom, so you assume that the current carried you 0.44 miles in these six minutes. This works out to a 4.4 knot current. In this case you can average, so add the two current rates and divide by two, and you get a 4 knot average for the current.

Now go back to your initial figures. You made one mile over the bottom on your upstream leg. You now know that you had a 4 knot current against you, and in 30 minutes this would have set you back 2 miles, so you made good 3 miles through the water rather than the 2.8 miles indicated by the log. The error is 7.3 per cent of the log reading.

On the downstream leg, you know you made a mile over the bottom, and that in six minutes the 4 knot current would have accounted for 0.4 miles of this distance, so your log should have read 0.60 rather than 0.56. This error—0.04 mile—is again 7.3 per cent of the log reading of 0.56. You now know that you must add 7.3 per cent to your log reading to get the actual distance travelled through the water. The same sort of calculations may be used to calibrate your speed indicator.

In actual practice, most logs are not graduated to anything finer than 0.5 miles, and you have to estimate anything beyond that. This means that you can get only a rough approximation of your log's error in a run of one mile, although it will do very well for a speed indicator if you power over the course and hold a steady speed. For really trustworthy calibration of your log, a longer run will be necessary—something over five miles. This means that the tidal currents will not remain constant while you sail a round trip to your mark and back. About the only way to beat this is to plan to start your run about two hours before slack water. In this way, you may be able to do your calibration during the period when there is least current running and hope that the small error introduced on one leg will approximately cancel out the error on the other leg.

The best way of checking your log is to do it while cruising. Read it whenever you pass a prominent landmark and make a note of the reading in your log. Read it again a few hours later when you can establish your position accurately. A few long runs such as this, with the current allowed for as well as you can from the charts and tables available to you, will soon tell you if there is any significant error in the log readings.

Keep the log head oiled frequently. If you routinely read it when you change watches, this is a good time to add a drop or two of oil. At the end of the season, I like to dismantle the head of the log and soak it for a day or two in kerosene to remove the gummy deposits of a season's oiling. I then dry it in alcohol, oil it lightly, and put it away for the winter.

If your log begins to register inaccurately, it is almost certainly due to wear in the ball bearings which carry the main drive shaft of the mechanism. These can be replaced very inexpensively, so don't buy a new log when a minor overhaul will do just as well. At the time that this is done, it is well to have the rubber gasket or sealing ring around the face of the log replaced. This rubber gets brittle and cracked after a few seasons, and no longer keeps the water out of the mechanism as it should.

The log line should be replaced every two to three seasons. This may well save you the expense of replacing the rotator as well. If your cruising takes you into game fish waters, you may find it worth while to use an idea I first heard of from Bob Van Blaricom of Sausalito, California. He lost a couple of rotators to sharks during an Atlantic crossing, and remedied the situation by inserting a five or six foot "leader" of $3/16$ inch stainless steel rigging wire just ahead of the rotator. He said that this made no apparent difference in the readings of the log, and definitely stopped the consumption of rotators.

This is a good place to suggest attaching a safety line from the log head to a deck fitting. One good strike from a big fish could very easily pull the mounting plate loose from the rail and result in your losing the entire log assembly.

Echo sounders require very little in the way of calibration, and usually are extremely stable once they are installed. The only exception is the type which has a rotating indicator arm carrying a small neon bulb which flashes to indicate the depth. The motor driving this arm may vary in speed, and this will markedly affect the accuracy of the soundings. Most manufacturers have fairly well solved this problem, but any set of bearings will wear in time, and if you use your sounder much, it would be well to check it from time to time. This matter of bearing wear from use does not apply to the type of sounder which uses a meter for an indicator, since the wear on the meter's jeweled bearings is negligible.

The easiest and most reliable means of checking your echo sounder is to let the boat drift while you drop a lead line over the side. Mark the lead line when it is straight up and down and read the sounder at the same time. Haul the line in and read it carefully. Shift the boat to another depth and repeat the procedure. The critical measurements, of course, are the ones in shallow water, although accurate readings in deeper water will allow you to do some nice navigating by bottom contours.

When checking your echo sounder in shallow water, measure the lead line carefully and take your measurements from a selected point on the rail of the boat. Note these depth measurements along with the corresponding sounder readings. The next time you slip your yacht, measure the distance vertically from this mark on the rail to the lowest point on the keel. With this data you can convert your lead line depths to depths of water *under the keel*, which is what you are really concerned with in shallow anchorages. A small correction chart for these shallower readings can be posted near the echo sounder, unless there is a zero adjustment on the instrument. In this case, you can adjust the sounder to indicate the depth under the keel and not have to do any mental arithmetic while you are nosing around in shoal waters.

Three things can make the rotating type of echo sounder read deeper than the water actually is, and this after all is the dangerous direction for any error. The first is wear and dirt in the bearings of the motor, which tend to slow it down. The second is weak batteries which will tend to make the motor run at reduced speed. The third is unusually cold water. The colder the water, the more slowly it conducts sound, and in extremely cold water, this will give an appreciable error in indicated depth. This works out to only about 0.4 per cent per degree Centigrade, so the actual error in shallow water will be very small. Unfortunately, extremely cold weather may also tend to slow down the rotor, and it is possible for these to summate to a significant figure. Just remember that if you should cruise in unusually cold fresh water in cold weather, it is well to allow for a little more depth than your yacht actually draws.

The Sextant. An excellent discussion of standard sextant adjustments is to be found in Bowditch * as well as in Mixter. If you own and use a sextant, you will probably have one or both of these books, so I shall not bother to repeat what they say so well. I have one comment to make, however, about a practice which may be relatively widespread among yachtsmen. Numerous yachtsmen have told me that they make a practice of adjusting their sextants so that the index error exactly compensates for the dip, thus eliminating the need to correct for anything other than altitude when a sight is taken.

I can readily appreciate the appeal of any measure that will save time for the yachting navigator, since he is usually the owner-skipper with a hundred other things to think of in addition to the navigation. At the same time, I see a very definite disadvantage to this procedure.

One can make very valuable use of the sextant for the measurement of horizontal angles, and these give a much more accurate fix than can be had from compass bearings. In this case, no dip correction is involved, and one is very likely to forget to account for the built-in index error which is customarily left out of one's computations.

Another fairly common practice seems to be to use a routine altitude correction of $+12'$, assuming that this covers everything except the correction for dip. It is true that this will work *reasonably* well for *most* of your sights, but not for all of them. Even if one confines all sights to altitudes between $12°$ and $60°$, the altitude corrections for the sun's lower limb vary from $+11.9'$ to $+15.7'$. This makes an error of $3.7'$ quite possible, and that means an error in position of 3.7 miles —considerably more than one ought to settle for. It takes such a short time to take out the correction for the actual altitude observed, that I see no justification for the use of an approximate rule of thumb.

UPPER AND LOWER SPREADER LIGHTS

The usual arrangement of spreader lights is very helpful when you are working in things at deck level, but can be a real hindrance when your work involves fouled halyards or anything above the level of the spreaders. A great improvement can be achieved by mounting a second set, controlled by a separate switch, on the upper surface of the

* Nathaniel Bowditch, *American Practical Navigator* (H.O. No. 9, U.S. Navy Hydrographic Office, 1958).

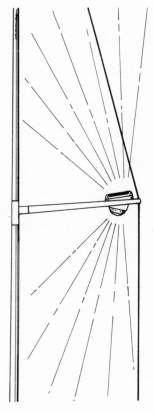

Fig. 62—Upper and lower spreader lights.

spreaders to illuminate the rigging and upper portion of the mast and sail. With the lower set turned off, these upper spreader lights give you an excellent view of everything aloft with no light in your eyes to blind you. (See Figure 62.)

If you wish to use commercially available light units, make sure that the ones intended for use as the upper set do not collect water around the edge of the glass lens, or you will soon have trouble with rusting and shorting out of this circuit. It is possible to make a set of lights for very little money, which are at least as satisfactory for this purpose as the quite expensive ones sold commercially.

Choose two sets of automobile dome lights or interior lights, making sure that the metal parts are stainless steel or brass. These should be of slightly different types, so I'll describe the upper set of lights first.

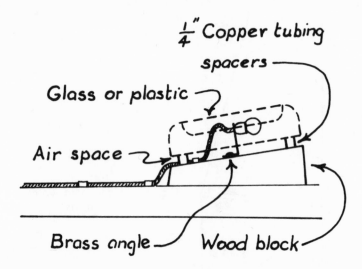

Fig. 63—Details of upper spreader light.

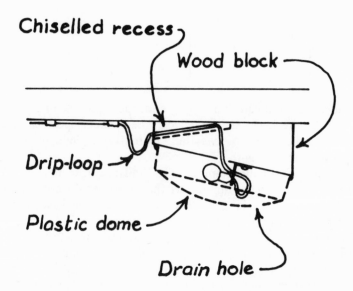

Fig. 64—Details of lower spreader light.

The fixtures should have a metal shell with a glass or plastic lens, as shown in Figure 63. There should be a metal base or bottom to the shell, and this can be supported from the wooden mounting block by wood screws and short spacers of copper tubing. Drill some holes in the metal bottom of the fixture to provide for good drainage. Mount the light at a slight angle so it will best illuminate the mast and rigging. You can try to seal the glass to the metal shell, but this is very difficult to do. It is more practical to assume that some water will get into the fixture and to provide for its rapid and complete drainage as shown in the drawing.

For the lower set, choose a fixture which has a dome shaped plastic lens, and mount it as shown in Figure 64. A drip loop in the wire will help to keep water from running in along the wire, while a small hole drilled at the low point of the plastic dome will permit the drainage of any water that does enter the fixture. Again, design the mounting blocks with an angle to direct the light in towards the center of the deck.

Connect the upper lights on one circuit and the lower ones on another, each with its own fuse and switch. In this way, they can be used simultaneously if you wish to make your presence known to an approaching ship, but can be operated independently for deck work. You will find the upper pair especially nice for looking at your masthead telltale at night, when you are running before the wind.

VI
INTERIORS

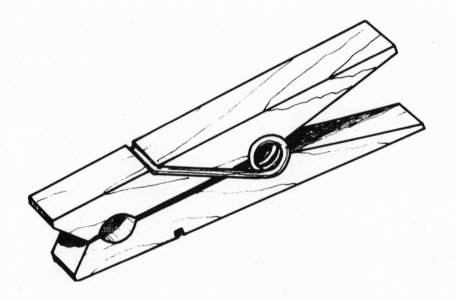

A HAND-THROUGH HATCH TO THE COCKPIT

A small opening cut through the bulkhead between the cockpit and the doghouse can be a real bonanza for the cook as well as the helmsman. (See Figure 65.) It serves as a means of conversing with the helmsman in bad weather without opening the companionway doors to the rain, and it enables the cook to pass hot drinks and sandwiches out to the cockpit without being drenched. In good weather, it can be left open for additional ventilation in the galley and to keep the cook from feeling cut off from the helmsman.

The opening should be just large enough to pass the largest dish you are likely to use—ten inches wide should be ample. The door, made from well-sealed marine plywood, slides in extruded plastic channels, although hardwood strips with grooves routed in them would

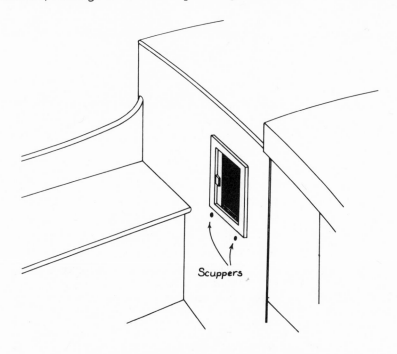

Fig. 65—"Hand-through" hatch to cockpit.

do as well. There is sufficient friction in this arrangement to keep the door closed without a fastening.

The frame for the door, containing the slides, should be assembled with waterproof glue and well painted or varnished inside. It is then set in place in bedding compound or thick varnish. Half-inch holes are drilled upward and inward through the bulkhead to serve as drains at each corner of the door slides.

A PELICAN HOOK TABLE MOUNTING

The saloon table is still one of the least satisfactory pieces of equipment in a sailing yacht. If it is conveniently situated for eating, it is inevitably in the way between meals. The gimballed, gyrating, telescoping monstrosities that have been developed in an effort to solve this problem are many and frightening to behold. Watching one of these things unfolding from its hiding place led an old friend of mine to remark, with passion, "That thing is the product of a diseased mind!"

A fairly conventionally designed table still seems to be best, if some provision can be made to change its location when you wish. The mounting shown here does a creditable job of this, and is easy and straightforward to install. It is copied from the usual gadget for holding steamship lounge chairs and dining chairs in place in bad weather.

Obtain an adjustable pelican hook from your chandler—the type often used for life lines and which incorporates a length adjustment similar to half a turnbuckle. Mount this hook from the underside of the table pedestal in such a fashion that the pelican hook, when closed, just reaches the cabin sole. On a table of a different design from that shown in the sketch, it may be necessary to use a length of chain to permit the hook to reach the cabin sole.

Let into the cabin sole two or more of the flush type lifting rings shown in the sketch (Figure 66), locating these where you wish to be able to place the table. The sections of cabin sole involved should be amply strong and well-supported by floor timbers. If necessary, these sections may be stiffened with some plywood pads on their undersurfaces in the way of the lifting rings. The sole sections should then be securely fastened down. I strongly recommend the use of large *stainless steel* wood screws for this. They will not freeze into the floor

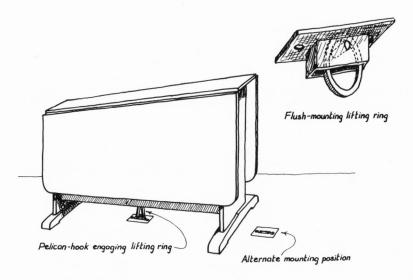

Flush-mounting lifting ring

Pelican-hook engaging lifting ring

Alternate mounting position

Fig. 66—Pelican hook mounting for saloon table.

timbers and can be easily removed if you wish to lift the cabin sole sections.

The pelican hook should be adjusted so that it can *just* be closed with some effort. Additional security can be had by cementing rubber pads to the bottoms of the table feet. The saloon carpeting can be slit to allow access for the lifting rings when the table is moved. A similar ring in the cockpit or on deck would permit the table to do double duty when you are lying in harbor.

FUEL STORAGE FOR OIL LAMPS

For a soft friendly light conducive to conversation and the enjoyment of a good meal, oil lamps are hard to beat. They are free from the annoying harshness of nearly all saloon fixtures of the electrical type, and, on chilly evenings, provide just enough heat to keep the cabin warm and comfortable. At night when underway, if turned down low, they allow one to move about without fumbling and still permit people to go on sleeping on the saloon settees.

Their biggest shortcoming is the odor which sometimes pervades a boat in which they are used. This can be nearly eliminated if the wicks are kept properly trimmed and if the lamps are filled without spilling fuel—no mean trick in a seaway if one has to use the usual funnel and kerosene can.

The plastic "squeeze bottles" now available make ideal fuel containers. If you get the type with a small spout or nozzle on the cap, the contents can be squeezed into a lamp without spilling a drop, even in the worst weather. We find the six ounce size best for our lamps, since one bottle just fills a lamp nicely.

We carry a dozen of these bottles in a wooden rack, as shown in Figure 67, and we find that this gives us a week's supply of oil under normal cruising conditions. This rack is mounted in an otherwise rather useless corner of the saloon, and has done away with shouts of "Where is the kerosene can?" and "Where did you put the funnel?", to say nothing of "Bring me a rag, quickly!"

Incidentally, filling and caring for the lamps is a responsibility that can often be assigned to one of the youngsters or less enthusiastic members of the crew. It gives them a sense of contributing something, and with these plastic blottles, a messy job is downright difficult to achieve.

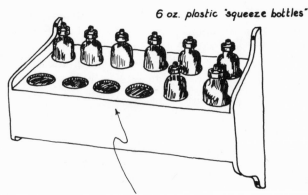

6 oz. plastic "squeeze bottles"

loose-fitting holes in upper shelf of wooden rack

Fig. 67—Fuel storage for oil lamps.

A REMOVABLE DISH RACK

Another idea for which I am indebted to Joe Cronk is this very ingenious stowage space for dishes and silverware. He has built it in, under the side deck, in *Jane Louise's* galley. Now, I'll admit there is nothing novel about this location, nor about the idea of a rack for plates and other dishes. What I admire about this bit of galley detail is the fact that the whole rack, including the silverware drawer, slides out when the two turn buttons at the sides are released. (See Figure 68.)

This not only makes cleaning it much easier for Joe's· wife, Mary, but it also means that it is possible to paint and varnish this rack when it gets scratched up and worn, and to do the work out where Joe can sand it properly and see what he is doing when he paints it. I am sure that sheer inaccessibility accounts for the sorry state of so many galley shelves and cupboards.

Joe made two hardwood arms which he attached, cantilever fashion, to the frames. These arms support hardwood runners on which the whole storage unit slides If one were to install this sort of unit next to a bulkhead, only one cantilevered support would be necessary, the other side being supported by a runner screwed to the bulkhead. If this is being incorporated in a new boat, the cantilever arms can be

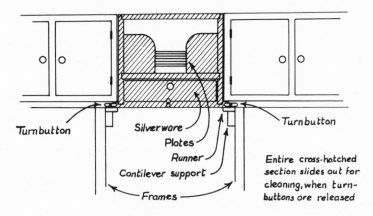

Fig. 68—Removable dish rack.

bolted to the frames before the ceilings are put in place, thus simplifying the installation by a good deal.

This idea will have to be modified, of course, for each specific installation, but the basic concept of securely held, yet removable, stowage compartments has a lot to be said for it, and can be adapted to numerous different stowage problems.

A PROPER SINK FOR A CRUISING SAILBOAT

Many attractive and well made stainless steel sinks are now available, and nearly all of these are quite practical for the motor cruiser, and perhaps even for the racing sailboat. I have yet to see one that is really suitable for a cruising sailboat, and this evaluation has to do entirely with the location and arrangement of the drains.

The motor cruiser may roll a good deal, but it never remains at a fixed angle of heel for any appreciable length of time. The racing sailboat certainly heels, but its tacks are likely to be relatively short and the emphasis not basically on creature comfort to begin with. In contrast, the cruising sailboat may be heeled over on the same tack for days at a time, and it can become very annoying to have to bail out the last quart of water that accumulates in the corner of the sink below the level of the drain outlet.

Stainless steel is a very difficult material to work, and the fabrication of a single sink of a special design is too difficult to undertake in the average yachtsman's own workshop and too expensive to have done professionally. On the other hand, an equally satisfactory and attractive sink can be made from fiberglass, and this material can easily be handled by the boat owner himself.

The design shown in the sketch will drain at almost any angle of heel through one or the other of the two outlets. Study your available space and carefully draw some full size plans before you begin your sink. Ideally, it would be desirable to have the walls curve inward slightly at the top to stop any slopping that might result from the rolling of the yacht. This, unfortunately, requires the use of a very complicated mould, and is not worth the additional trouble. Almost the same results can be achieved by keeping the sink relatively deep.

To facilitate removing the mould when the plastic has set, the sides of the sink will have to slope outward a very slight amount. Three degrees from the vertical will be ample, if you take the trouble to get a good smooth finish on the surface of the mould.

Get some stainless steel drains, complete with strainers and stoppers from your plumbing supplier. At the same time get a "Y" joint of tubing the same diameter as the drain tubes. If your dealer cannot supply this, have it made from some brass or stainless steel tubing, and have a "T" added below the "Y" as shown in the drawing (Figure 69a). Re-

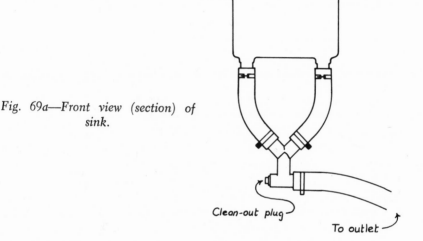

Fig. 69a—Front view (section) of sink.

Clean-out plug

To outlet

moving the plug in the "T" will allow you to shove a length of wire rope through the drain and right out the through-hull fitting, if the drain ever clogs.

Make the mould from some easily worked wood such as white pine. Start by making a box sufficiently thick to allow you to round the corners as much as you wish. With a male mould such as this, you get a beautiful finish on coved corners, and they will be very much easier to clean than a corner of small curvature. Make the bottom of the mould sloping toward the front of the sink at least ten degrees, as shown in the drawing of the side view (Figure 69b.) Then, even if the boat is out of trim fore and aft, the sink will still drain properly. Avoid using nails or screws when making the mould. Glue will hold well enough, and you'll not have to worry about hitting a nail with your plane when you are shaping the mould.

Sand the mould well and give it a coat of flat paint. Fill all surface

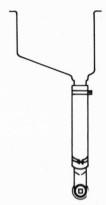

Fig. 69b—Side view of sink. Note how the bottom slopes toward the drains.

irregularities with trowel cement and sand again. Repeat this until you have as perfect a surface as you can get, then give it a coat of enamel. When this is dry, sand it lightly with *very* fine paper.

Set this mould upside down on a flat square of plywood a few inches larger than the mould all around. Fasten it in place with a few nails from the bottom, and fill the crack between the mould and the plywood with trowel cement. Try to finish this to a rounded corner with a radius of about ¼ inch. Tack some ¼ inch square strips of wood to the plywood to form a border or frame 1 inch out from the sides of the mould. Paint and sand this base section, and give the entire mould a couple of coats of parting agent, obtainable from your plastics supplier. (See Figure 70.)

Set the drain fixtures in place on the bottom of the mould, and fasten them down with long wood screws to hold them securely in position while the fiberglass is laminated.

If you have had no experience in moulding fiberglass, ask your supplier for his advice as to the correct materials to buy as well as for detailed instructions for their use. Follow these instructions carefully, especially where mixing proportions and curing times and temperatures are concerned. Each different resin has its own characteristics, so it is impossible to give the exact directions here, but the following general outline will be enough, if accompanied by the information from your supplier.

First, give the entire mould a coat of gelcoat in the color you have chosen for the sink. When this has set, you may wish to apply a second colored gelcoat to reduce the likelihood of scratches ever showing

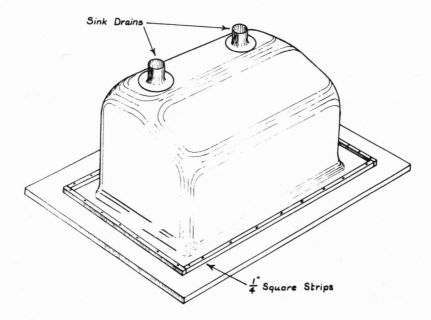

Sink Drains

¼" Square Strips

Fig. 70—Wooden sink mould ready for the laying up of the fiberglass.

the base color through the finish. When the last gelcoat has cured to the proper point, lay up the first fiberglass lamination. Carry the cloth well up onto the necks of the drain fittings, and reinforce these with collars of glass cloth cut to fit over the tubes. Two or three layers of cloth or glass matting will be ample. Be sure you wet the glass thoroughly with the resin and work out all air bubbles as you go.

When the finished laminate has had ample time to set, remove it from the mould. This can be started by tapping over the outer surface of the fiberglass with a mallet, hard enough to start it away from the mould but not hard enough to damage it. If your parting agent has been properly applied, it should not be difficult to get the sink to release.

Trim off the excess from the flanges, using a coarse sanding disk in an electric drill. Avoid sanding the gelcoat where it will be exposed when the sink is installed. Gelcoat can be applied with a brush to touch up defects, but it will not have the same fine surface finish that it receives from a well-finished mould.

Mount the sink, bedding it in bedding compound or a rubber sealing material. The flange may be drilled and countersunk for mounting screws, and it will definitely pay you to use stainless steel screws here.

The hoses for the drains can often be had from an auto supply with the desired degree of curvature already moulded into the rubber. This eliminates any tendency for the hose to collapse at the bends. Ask to see an assortment of radiator hoses and choose those that most nearly correspond to the shape you need. Use stainless steel hose clamps. They are less expensive in the long run and are always easy to remove when you wish to replace the hose.

Attach the drain stoppers, by their chain, to the sink or drainboard with wood or metal screws. If you decide to attach them to the sink walls, drill a hole through the fiberglass and use a machine screw with fiber washers and a nut.

I can assure you that the time spent in making this sink will earn you a vote of thanks from your cook.

THE CLOTHESPIN AT SEA

Our first use of spring-type clothespins aboard Viking "S" was for the rather unimaginative purpose of hanging out the wash. They actually work very well for this, even in a good wind, since we usually hang the laundry on the plastic covered life lines. These are large enough to give the pins a good grip, and the plastic eliminates any possibility of rust marks.

It wasn't long, however, until my wife was out buying another box of the clothespins. Not that we had larger washes, but the things began to be used for so many other purposes that there was always a chronic shortage of them for the laundry. Incidentally, we always keep a dozen or so pins clipped to a length of cord hanging in the galley. They are instantly available and easy enough to replace, and we always know where we can find one in a hurry.

Varnished, and then tacked to a bulkhead, they make excellent clips for navigational notes, shopping lists, weather station frequencies and times, letters to be mailed, etc. By separating the two parts of the pin, one can tack one half flat against a bulkhead with small copper nails and then reassemble the clothespin. It makes a neat and secure mounting for any number of things.

We use plastic bags a great deal for food stowage, especially for anything such as cheese, sausage, salad greens, etc., which we wish to keep from drying out. The clothespin seems to be the ideal fastener for these bags. Just roll the neck a few times and clamp a clothespin on it. This also works well for protecting delicate instruments, cameras, etc. from salt spray.

A clothespin clipped to your charting pencil near the end does not interfere with your use of the pencil, but it does keep it from rolling off the chart table. Another clothespin tacked to the bulkhead makes an excellent holder for the pencil, when it is not in use, and a couple of the clothespins mounted with their jaws up make a good holder for parallel rules.

Clothespins can often serve as a third hand for the assembly of a dismantled instrument or engine part, since they will grip a nut or part quite securely. Two or three of them can be snapped together to form a sort of tripod to position a small part, freeing your hands for the rest of the task. I have often improvised a holder for a flash light by clipping several clothespins on a fuel line or other engine part.

A couple of years ago I was doing some coach-whipping on a bit of rigging, and I was faced with the problem of keeping track of eight long strands of marline. I found that clothespins made excellent bobbins for this. If the marline was wound around the clothespin in figure-of-eight turns, the pin could still be opened enough to grip the last turn and prevent its unrolling. I could quickly pull it free and unroll a few inches whenever I wished and the marline was always short enough to handle easily. By numbering these bobbins with a pencil, one can keep track of the strands in fancy knot work.

Clothespins make excellent clamps for small glue jobs, and are good for holding parts to be soldered when you do not wish the heat to be conducted away from the parts. I also find them useful for holding temporary electrical connections while I test a circuit.

I am sure that this list can be expanded many fold by others who have come to rely on this humble gadget for dozens of jobs afloat. Keep a good supply on board. The plastic type is good if you do not wish to bother with paint or varnish. Perhaps the most important thing is to get pins with well galvanized or plated springs, as these always seem to be the first parts to succumb to the salt air.

VII
GROUND TACKLE

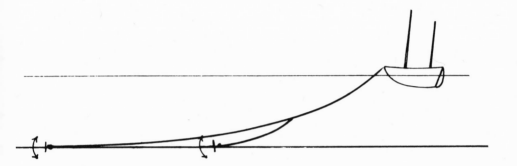

CHAIN STOPPER

Your anchor windlass is an expensive and very useful piece of machinery, but it is intended to aid in getting in the anchor and not to serve as a mooring bit. When the anchor is down and you have veered enough chain, the chain should be stopped off to take the strain off the windlass pawl. The stopper shown here will enable you to do this quickly and securely, yet it can be cast off in a moment if you should suddenly wish to take in or veer more chain, and you need no pliers or shackle key to operate it.

It is made from a length of stainless steel rod a little larger in diameter than the material from which your chain links are formed. I used ½ inch rod for my ⅜ inch chain. It should be bent to the shape shown and the eye should be securely welded. Be certain to heat the rod when you bend it. It should be stronger than your chain, and cold bending stainless steel to these small radius curves materially weakens the bend.

The spacing of the jaws of the hook is important. The gap should be just wide enough to pass easily over a chain link, and the throat should be well rounded so there is no tendency for the chain to jam under a load. The angle shown in Figure 71 will give a nice fairlead under tension.

This stopper hook is attached by a chain or wire strop to an eye bolt in the deck. This eye bolt should be sufficiently strong and well enough backed up with pads under the beams to take the full strain of the anchor. Mine fastens to the deck fitting for the heel of my bowsprit, as described on page 42.

After the anchor is set and the chain's length adjusted to suit the depth of water, the stopper is dropped over a chain link and the windlass brake is released. It is wise, after allowing enough chain to run to put the strain on the stopper, to re-engage the windlass clutch so it is ready for instant use.

These stoppers can serve many useful purposes. For example, I always carry an extra one in my shackle bucket to use on the end of a length of nylon line for handling other people's anchor chains on which I have become fouled. They grip securely, but can be released in an instant.

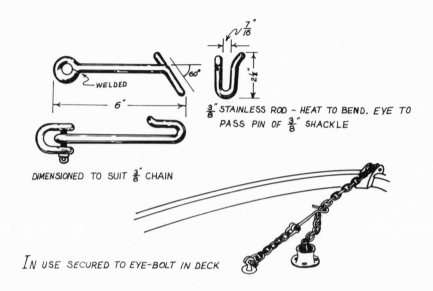

Fig. 71—Chain stopper.

TRIPPING LINE

In a crowded anchorage, and certainly in any Mediterranean harbor, a tripping line by which you can lift your anchor when it fouls can save a great deal of exertion and frustration. Buoying it, however, no longer seems to be advisable. If a power boat doesn't foul it, someone is likely to come in and moor to the buoy with fairly obvious results. If you are spared these complications, some enterprising youngster in a skiff is almost certain to add it to his collection of "things found floating" (which of course it *is*), and take it along to sell it.

We bend a light nylon tripping line into the eye at the crown of the anchor, and then carry this line back along the chain, seizing it to the chain every five or six feet and finally stopping its end to the chain (Figure 72). When we go to raise the anchor, even if someone has laid a chain over ours, we can usually pick up our chain with a boat hook and work our way out to where I can get hold of the tripping line. It is then a simple matter to break the light cotton stopping loose and use the tripping line to lift the anchor to the deck where I can unshackle the chain and bring it in freely.

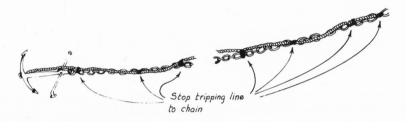

Fig. 72—*Unbuoyed tripping line. Use light cotton twine for stoppings.*

If you use a brightly colored nylon line for this, it aids in recognizing your own anchor chain in a crowded harbor.

ANCHOR RELEASE

The shorthanded sailor will find this gadget a great help when anchoring. One man can handle a good-sized boat quite well under way, but he has his hands full entering a harbor. This is especially true if the anchor must be dropped at a particular spot, or if it is to be used to hold the bow off a quay when mooring stern-to, as is the universal practice in the Mediterranean.

Find an old D-shackle large enough to slip over your anchor chain easily. You'll not need the shackle pin for this, and if your shackle bucket is anything like mine, there are always a number of pinless shackles in it. Make a very loose fitting pin from rod stock, and bend an eye in one end. The pin should be four or five inches long and a very loose sliding fit in the shackle. (See Figure 73.)

When you approach the anchorage, hang off the anchor using this modified shackle as an anchor stopper. It can be kept secured to an eyebolt in the deck by a short strop or chain. Run a light line from the eye of the loose fitting shackle pin through a small block on the rail, and back to the cockpit.

When you are ready to let go the anchor, a jerk on the line slips the pin out of the shackle and the anchor runs free. Needless to say, in hanging off the anchor it is wise to check the windlass to make certain the brake is off and the chain ready to run free. If you employ a nylon warp with a short shot of chain on the anchor, you can use this release equally well. In this case, the coil of nylon can be brought

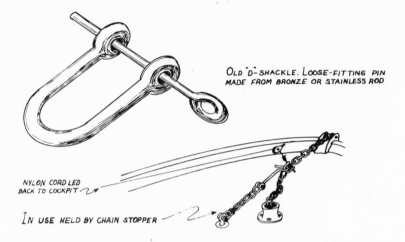

Fig. 73—Anchor release.

back to the cockpit where you can pay it out or snub it as you choose. Be certain that the eye and shackle where the rope joins the chain will pass through your anchor fairlead. If they will not, hang the shackle and eye over the side so they will not foul when the chain runs out.

ANCHORING AND ANCHOR ANGLES

Good discussions of ground tackle and its use are too plentiful for me to be tempted to add another. Instead, I shall make a few comments based on some years of experience on both American and English yachts where preferences in ground tackle do differ, and add a few tricks I have learned which enable one to get a little more out of the tackle at hand.

The American tendency to use nylon anchor warps with a short shot of chain ahead of the anchor certainly reduces the weight, when compared with the use of chain for the entire anchor rode. It also somewhat reduces the mess on the foredeck when the anchor is brought up from a dirty bottom, and it does away with the problems of rusting chain. After having used both chain and rope warps, however, I'll plump for chain every time for a cruising boat. It is much easier to stow. It runs out with no tendency to snarl or foul, and its weight greatly increases the holding power of any anchor.

The usual method of breaking out any anchor is to shorten the chain until the shank of the anchor is lifted up from the bottom and acts as a lever to pry the buried fluke or flukes out. Conversely, the holding power of any anchor can be increased by any method which will *prevent* the shank from being lifted up, and it is for this reason that the length of chain is usually used between the anchor and the nylon warp.

By adding a weight, such as a pig of ballast, to the warp, the holding power can be further increased, and the long low catenary curve of a chain anchor rode seems to do the best job of all. It is impossible to pull hard enough on fifteen or twenty fathoms of ⅜ inch chain to straighten it out. It will always hang in a curve, and this keeps the pull on the anchor nearly parallel to the bottom where it belongs.

No cruising boat should ever be equipped with only one anchor, but if I had to choose one type for the cruising boat, I should unhesitatingly settle on the old "fisherman" or "yachtsman's" anchor with a folding stock for easy stowing. The CQR "plow" would be my next choice. Seldom seen in America, it holds extremely well in mud or sand, cannot be fouled, and carries very well in a fairlead on the stem. (See Figure 74.)

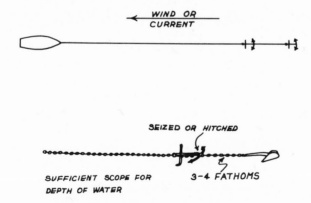

Fig. 74—Two anchors on same chain give holding power several times that of single anchor.

The Danforth-type anchor holds fantastically well for its weight, once it is set in the right kind of bottom. It will bury itself in mud and I have seen the flukes badly bent by the strain needed to break out a well-set Danforth from a clay bottom. Nevertheless, it too often fails to set at all for me to consider its use on a cruising boat.

Neither the Danforth nor the CQR is really satisfactory on a rock bottom, and they are hopeless on a bottom which has a heavy growth of weed. The fisherman, however, with its sharp flukes, cuts down through the weed and sets rather than just skating along over the top. Of all the styles of the fisherman, I like the Herreschoff pattern best. Its flukes are sharp enough to penetrate weed well and of sufficient area to hold well in sand or clay, and its weight is distributed where it is needed to make the anchor set and hold well.

In actual practice, I have found the combination of a CQR as a main anchor, carried on 45 fathoms of chain, and a fisherman with five fathoms of chain and a ¾ inch diameter nylon warp to be a very effective combination. The CQR works well in nearly all circumstances, and stows on my bowsprit. The fisherman works well in situations where I can't trust the CQR. The two together, rigged as shown in Figure 74, make a combination that is almost impossible to drag.

There are hundreds of tricks that can be used to make anchoring more convenient and reliable, and these make for fine arguments on winter evenings in the club. Perhaps the only universal rule to remember and to practice, even when you don't feel like it, is to do what has to be done *while you can still do it.* Laying out a second anchor can be an unwelcome chore when you are tired after a day's sailing, but it is much more of an ordeal with a high wind and a choppy sea in which to try to handle a dinghy.

Beyond veering more chain, the first added bit of holding power can be gained by running a weight down the chain on a roller in order to increase the catenary curve of the chain. This should be a good heavy weight of thirty or forty pounds, and a line should be bent to the roller so the weight can be hauled back aboard if it becomes necessary to get the anchor up.

The next degree of protection involves laying out an additional anchor, and this always involves the decision of how and where to lay it. In a restricted anchorage, one has to limit his swinging circle. Unfortunately, this is always in conflict with obtaining the greatest possible holding power. In Figure 75a, two anchors are arranged to limit

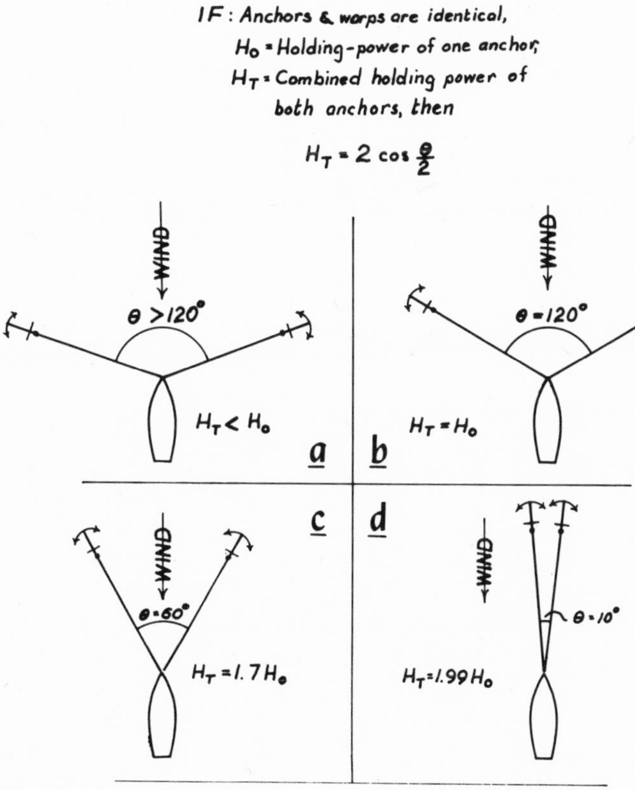

IF: Anchors & warps are identical,
H_0 = Holding-power of one anchor,
H_T = Combined holding power of
both anchors, then

$$H_T = 2 \cos \frac{\theta}{2}$$

$\theta > 120°$

$H_T < H_o$ **<u>a</u>** **<u>b</u>** $H_T = H_o$

$\theta = 120°$

<u>c</u> **<u>d</u>**

$\theta = 60°$

$H_T = 1.7 H_o$

$\theta = 10°$

$H_T = 1.99 H_o$

WIND

Fig. 75—Effect of angle on holding power.

the yacht's swing to a very small area. The same result could be obtained with one bow anchor and one stern anchor spread at the same
angle. The wide angle between the anchors markedly increases the
strain they have to resist. When the angle between them is more than
120°, with the wind direction as shown in the sketch, the two anchors
will actually hold less than one anchor straight out to windward.

If you doubt this, consider for a moment the result of swigging on
a halyard to set it up tightly. A sidewise pull on the halyard exerts
many times more force than pulling straight in line. Actually, assuming the two anchors to be identical, the chains of equal length, the
bottom homogeneous, and the wind direction as shown in the sketch,

their combined holding power (relative to that of either one taken individually) can be found by the formula:

$$H_t = 2 \cos \frac{\theta}{2}$$

where θ represents the included angle between the two anchor chains.

When the two anchors are separated by an angle of 120° (Figure 75b), the combined holding power is exactly equal to that of one of them out to windward. With 60° between the warps (Figure 75c), the holding power becomes 1.7 times that of a single anchor, while with 10° between the warps, the combined holding power of 1.99 times that of a single anchor (Figure 75d). You are now getting almost your money's worth in holding power from your second anchor.

There are times, however, when even this does not keep one from dragging. What can we do then, if we have only the two anchors? There are two approaches, and both accomplish the same general result. The first is a little easier to set up, in terms of foredeck work, although it does not give quite the holding power. It consists of dropping one anchor, veering perhaps fifteen fathoms of chain, then dropping a second anchor on a short shot of perhaps five fathoms of chain. The end of this is made fast to the main chain, as shown in Figure 76, and the main chain is veered to a total of twenty-five or thirty fathoms.

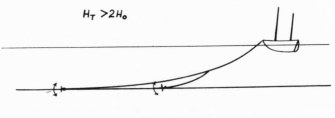

$H_T > 2H_o$

Fig. 76

This adds the weight of the second chain to that of the first and makes it much harder to break out the anchor at the end of the chain.

The method shown in Figure 74, was described to me by Arthur Roca, and is discussed by Jean Merrien, in his *Dictionnaire de la Mer.**

* Jean Merrien, *Dictionnaire de la Mer* (Paris: R. Laffront, 1958).

Merrien claims that this gives a holding power three times that of a single anchor of a weight equal to the combined weight of the two anchors used. I cannot vouch for the mathematical accuracy of this assertion, but I recently had an opportunity to try this method and I was amazed at the results. It not only stopped our dragging in the rather fierce wind which was blowing, but it refused to budge when I tested it by running our not insignificant engine full astern. It felt as if we were swinging to a battleship mooring, and I can heartily recommend it for situations where you need as much holding power as your ground tackle can be persuaded to give.

In this method, the second anchor, rather than being dropped on a short chain of its own, is shackled directly to the main chain five or six fathoms above the first anchor, and the chain is hitched or seized to its crown as shown in Figure 74. Two CQR anchors laid in this fashion should make an excellent mooring, because they will not foul the chain. If a fisherman is used, it should be checked frequently with this in mind. Fouling is only likely to occur in light winds when the yacht drifts around and around for a time.

VIII
CANVAS WORK
AND MARLINESPIKE
SEAMANSHIP

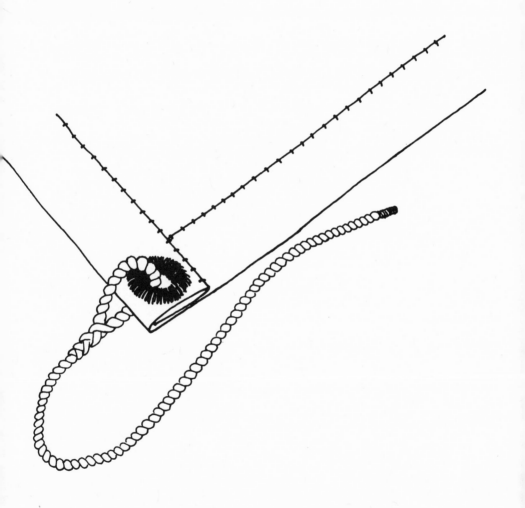

YACHT FENDERS

A cruising yacht seldom has enough of the heavy duty fenders she really needs, and always seems to lose a few during a sailing season. Here is a winter project which can provide you with a supply of sturdy, practical fenders at a very moderate cost.

There is nothing new about the idea of using tires for fenders—the fishermen do it all the time. The problem is one of avoiding the black marks tires make on a yacht's topsides. The usual drum-shaped canvas covers take careful cutting and sewing, and quickly wear through in spots. The method shown here has worked very well for me, is quick and easy to do, and gives three thicknesses of canvas cover.

I like to use the small tires used for motor scooters and mini-cars, and your tire dealer should be able to locate a number of these for you. Try to get tires whose walls are not too limp, so they will give plenty of protection to your yacht. In one edge of the tread cut two holes large enough to pass the line you wish to use for the fenders. A knife with a stiff blade and a sharp point works well for this. The holes should be about two inches apart to avoid weakening the tire too much. Directly opposite these holes, cut another hole for drainage of water which may get inside the casing when it is in use.

Use relatively heavy canvas for the cover. Your sailmaker may have some scraps which will do well for this purpose and which he will sell you cheaply. Cut the canvas into strips 6 inches wide. These should be cut at an angle to the weave of the cloth, as shown in the sketch. Your wife would say that they are cut "on the bias." Sew these together to make one long strip, 6 inches wide and long enough to cover a tire. To estimate the length needed, measure in inches the outside circumference of the tire and call this C. Measure the circumference of the tire's *cross section*, and call this c. Now, the length needed to cover the tire will be $(C/2)(c + 1)$.

Fold one edge of the strip over halfway, so that the strip is now 4 inches wide, and crease this fold in along the length of the strip. Roll the strip as if it were a bandage, with the narrow 2-inch fold showing on the outside of the roll and the doubled edge at your right as shown in Figure 77. If you keep track of the length of your first strip, and then subtract the length of the surplus you are left with when you

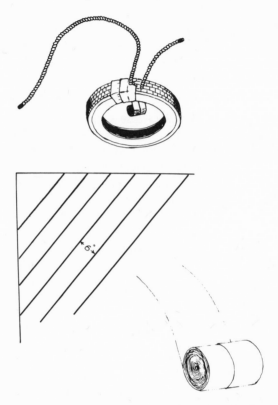

Fig. 77—Canvas cover for tire-casing fender.

have finished, you can arrive at a very close measure of the length needed for subsequent rolls.

Take a six or seven foot length of rope and stop both ends with constrictor knots (page 152). Pass one end through one of the pair of holes in the tire and back out through the other. Now begin winding on the "bandage." Wrap it as shown in the drawing, so that the 2-inch fold lies next to the tire and so that each turn exactly half covers the preceding turn. You can see the imprint of the 2-inch fold through the canvas—use this as a guide for the spacing. Since the canvas is cut on the bias, you can stretch it enough, "edgesetting" it as it were, to get a very nice fit. The exposed edge should be the doubled edge.

When your wrapping approaches the rope, have a knife handy. Wrap right up to the rope, and then slit the single thickness edge of the canvas as shown in Figure 77. The next turn should just miss the rope on the other side and will cover the slit as it does so. Finish wrapping the tire and sew the end of the canvas down securely.

Now arrange the rope so that about twelve inches of the left end is protruding. Unlay this and splice it into the other side, making an eye splice at the tire end. This should be as short as possible. Whip the other end of the rope, or put in another eye splice, depending on your favorite method of hanging your fenders.

The fenders may be painted if you wish, but it really isn't necessary. If you will take the time to cut a stencil, the name of your yacht can be stenciled on each by spraying with lacquer from a spray can.

These fenders are heavy enough to stay where you want them, even in a high wind, and they are tough enough to withstand real punishment. My wife discovered that one of these hung over the side from the shrouds makes a good substitute for the swimming ladder. Since that time, getting one hung off has been part of our "man overboard" drill.

SAFETY FASTENINGS FOR SUN AWNINGS

If it is to be at all enjoyable, summer cruising almost demands sun awnings. I suppose there are as many types of awnings as there are boat owners, but most of them rely on some sort of lanyards and guys to hold them in place. Transverse slats or poles resting on the boom are simple and effective, and with this arrangement the awning itself can be secured to the shrouds at one or more points.

Sudden, unexpected squalls are often overlooked when the awning fastenings are being designed and made. Every season I see some frantic scrambles as crews attempt to untie all kinds of complicated knots in awning lanyards—not an easy thing to do when the awning is being whipped around by a high wind. The time spent in making up the fastenings illustrated in Figure 78 will come back to you many fold. You can be relaxing on deck with your awning safely furled while your neighbors are still fighting with theirs.

The edge fastening, which attaches to the shroud, consists of two brass grommets spaced about two inches apart in the hem of the awning. In one of these, a loop of sash cord is secured with an overhand knot above and below the grommet. One leg of the loop is cut off

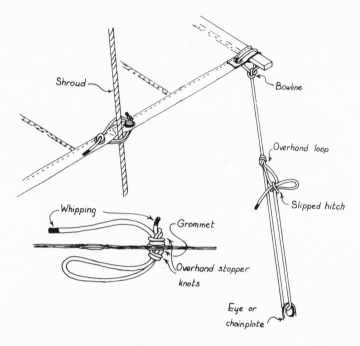

Fig. 78—Awning fastenings.

close and whipped. The other is left about ten inches long, with its end whipped. The bight should be just long enough to pass around the shroud and up through the other grommet, where it is toggled in place with the ten inch leg. A quick pull removes the toggle, and the loop can be flipped out of the grommet and free. Modifications of this fastening can be applied to many articles aboard the yacht.

The fastening for the guy line has an overhand loop tied about half way down to deck level. The end of the line is passed through a deck fitting, back up through this loop, and belayed with a slipped hitch. A quick jerk on the end of the line slips the hitch, and the guy may be pulled free. This arrangement allows you to adjust the tension as you like it, and still be able to get the awning down at a moment's notice.

A SAIL BAG LANYARD

I lost three sail bags into the drink before I devised this very simple remedy. Now I find I have not only stopped losing sail bags, but sail changing has become easier, since I have one less thing to think about.

I sewed a reinforcing patch in the center of the bottom of the sail bags. Any shape will do, but make it four or five inches across. I next worked a grommet into this patch, sewing it over a marline grommet (see page 160). I happen to like these made grommets, although a brass eyelet would do just as well. I then made up the lanyard from ¼-inch diameter nylon, eye-splicing the nylon line into bronze snaps of the dog-leash type. These snaps should be fairly large so that they may easily be snapped to a variety of fittings.

The lanyard is then cut to about four feet long, and the end foot and a half is unlaid and a Matthew Walker knot is tied in it. The strands are laid up again and stuck through the grommet in the bottom of the sail bag. Inside the bag, the lanyard is secured by a stopper knot such as a doubled wall and crown. (See Figure 79.)

Now, when you arrive on deck with a headsail to change, snap the lanyard to a shroud or life line, and you can forget about the sail bag. It is easy to pull the sail out of the bag, and the bag will not blow away. It is securely fastened to the yacht, and moreover by the bottom, so it will not fill with wind and thrash around.

When you get ready to hand a sail, snap its bag to a lifeline and

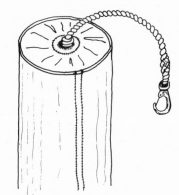

Fig. 79—Safety lanyard on sailbag.

you can forget about it until you need it. You will find this little wrinkle vastly reduces the tendency to stuff the headsail down the hatch unbagged in bad weather.

THE CONSTRICTOR KNOT

I have met relatively few yachtsmen who know and use Ashley's Constrictor Knot, although H. G. Smith has a very good discussion of it in his *Arts of The Sailor*, and, of course, it is amply displayed in Ashley's own monumental work, *The Ashley Book of Knots*. Since it is such a useful knot, and does a job not really done by any other knot I know of, I want to present it here in the hope that it will eventually gain the popularity it deserves. It really should be one of the first five or six knots a yachtsman learns.

Ashley invented this knot for a very specific purpose—to serve in place of a seizing or whipping. It does this very well, holding like a vise on any rounded object such as a spar, rope, the neck of a bag, etc. One word of caution is in order, however. The slipped version of this knot can be untied very easily, but the unslipped version is almost impossible to untie, so it is best used where you expect to have to cut it off just as you would a seizing. I find it invaluable as a seizing on strands of a rope to be spliced, and I routinely use it when I am cutting and splicing wire rope. Once the knot has been pulled up tight, the strand can be cut with no danger of its unlaying.

The constrictor knot is nothing more than a half knot with a round turn over the top of the crossing, as you can see in Figure 80. To tie it on a spar or in the middle of a rope, make a round turn as shown in Figure 80a, crossing back over toward the left as if you were going to tie a clove hitch. Then bring the end up *over* the standing part and then under the two crossing parts as shown in Figure 80b. Pulled down tight it will look like Figure 80c. The secret of the knot lies in the fact that both ends emerge through the V-shaped openings between crossed strands. The more tightly the knot is pulled, the more tightly these crossed strands grip the ends. As Ashley says, "it has a ratchet-like grip," and can be adjusted to just the degree of tightness you wish. It is much faster than using seizings when splicing, and is perfectly secure if tied with small stuff on a round or convex object,

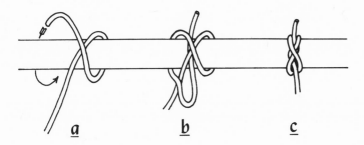

Fig. 80—*The constrictor knot tied on middle section of spar or rope.*

where the shape of the object forces the half knot up against the over-riding round turn.

The knot may be tied very quickly over the end of a rope or spar, as shown in Figure 81, and this is the best way to tie it when seizing

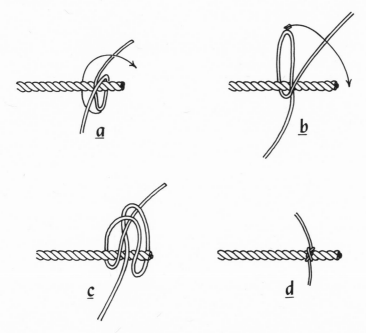

Fig. 81—*The constrictor knot tied over the end of a spar or rope.*

the end of a rope strand or using it for a whipping. Take a round turn, as shown in Figure 81a. Then reach over the round turn and pull out some slack in the bight. Bring this bight over the top of the crossed ends and down over the end of the rope, as shown in Figures 81b and 81c. Drawn tight, it looks like Figure 81d, and the ends may be cut off close up to the knot.

There are a couple of useful variations to this knot. If, instead of tucking the *end* as shown in Figure 80, you tuck a *bight* as shown in Figure 82a, the result is the Slipped Constrictor. Drawn down it looks like Figure 82b. It holds very well, but can be instantly released by slipping the bight. This makes it an excellent knot for closing the mouths of bags. I have also used it for hitching lanyards to shrouds and stays, although it is not as good for this purpose as a slipped rolling hitch.

If, instead of taking a single crossing turn as shown in Figure 80a, you take two turns as shown in Figure 83a, the result will be the Double Constrictor. Drawn down, it looks like Figure 83c, and is a half knot with two round turns over it. It is more difficult to draw this knot down tight, but once it is pulled down properly it can be used as a semi-permanent whipping at the end of a line, even if the ends of the constrictor are cut off close.

An evening spent learning this knot and its variations can be a very good investment. As I say, I would include it among the five or six basic knots a yachtsman should know, and in view of this I find it very interesting that this knot—simple as it is—has not been known for

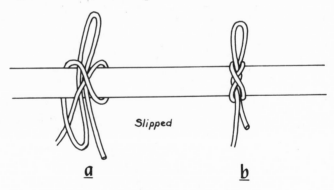

Fig. 82—Slipped constrictor knot.

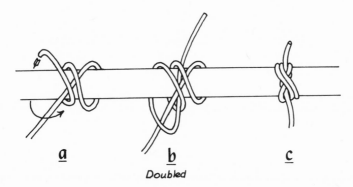

Fig. 83—Double constrictor knot.

hundreds of years, but was invented just a few years ago—long after the great sailing ships had disappeared.

COCKPIT DODGERS

Each additional year finds me more capable of appreciating the advantages of an enclosed steering station. Driving to weather can be exhilarating for a short while, but when you are faced with it for a long period, it becomes just another unpleasant interlude. Not all yachts lend themselves to enclosed steering positions, even of a temporary nature, but it is surprising how much comfort you can get from a pair of simple dodgers lashed to the life lines, and these can be rigged on almost any boat. (See Figure 84.) They are easy and quick to put up and take down, and require hardly any stowage space.

These dodgers are ideal items to begin with, if you would like to learn something about canvas work, and I know you will get a great

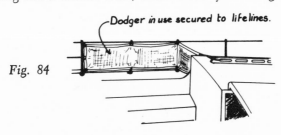

Fig. 84

deal of use from them. I made ours three years ago while we were making a passage—I like to do canvas work when we are under way—and we have used them on almost every cruise since then. I shall assume you have had no experience at canvas work or sailmaking, and describe this as a sort of introductory exercise. Even if you are an old hand at needle work, you will find the dodgers well worth making. Just skip the detailed instructions.

Canvas is much easier to work with than dacron or nylon. If this is your first project, use canvas and try your hand with synthetic fabrics later. Get a good grade of canvas sail cloth, and get it fairly heavy since these dodgers take a lot of punishment in heavy weather. Twelve ounce cotton canvas (by American reckoning) will be about right. American sail cloth usually comes 28 inches wide, and one width of this should be adequate for most yachts.

My dodgers run fore and aft along the lifelines for six feet, and then angle in across the side deck to attach to the side of the doghouse at their forward ends. Decide how long you wish to make yours, and make your pattern accordingly. In Figure 85, the length A of the larger

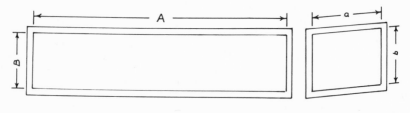

Fig. 85

piece should be the desired finished length. The height B should be approximately equal to the distance from the rail cap to the life lines (upper). Draw a light pencil line on your deck where the forward portion will angle in to the doghouse, and measure this line to get *a*, the length of the shorter forward section. The angle is to allow for the camber of the deck, and you can measure this with an adjustable bevel or by cutting a cardboard pattern.

Make your patterns from these measurements, allowing an additional 1½ inches all the way around for seams and *tablings*, as the sailmaker is wont to call a hem. Mark this on the canvas with a lead pencil, using the selvage of the canvas as the outside line wherever possible. Cut out the canvas pieces with a sharp knife or heavy scissors.

Draw a pencil line around each piece 1½ inches in from the edge. Now draw a second line one inch inside this, and just to keep things straight, mark the second line with red pencil, making sure the pencil is not a water soluble one. This red line will be useful when you begin to stitch the tablings.

Take a look at Figure 86, which shows the steps in making a tabling. Lay the large piece of canvas out with the red line up, and make a ½ inch wide fold along the after end, folding the edge in toward the red line. Crease this fold in with a knife handle or a seam rubber if you have one. Now fold this edge again, so that the crease you have just made lies along the red line. Crease it again along this second fold. It should now look like Figure 86a. To hold this fold in place, the sailmaker uses sail needles for pins. This always makes a hump in the cloth which tends to throw your stitching off and it is a pretty lethal arrangement if you happen to drag your hand across the row of needles. It is much easier and more satisfactory to staple this fold in with an

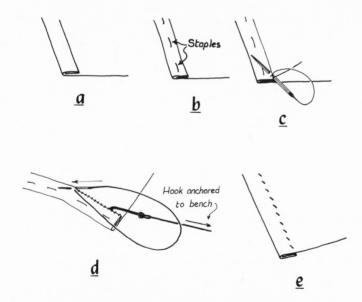

Fig. 86—Steps in making a "tabling."

ordinary stapling machine, placing your staples three or four inches apart down the center of the folded tabling as shown in Figure 86b. If you use staples for assembling the pieces later, and they work very well indeed, think it through carefully. Place the staples from the side that will be exposed when the seam is finished. Then you will be able to get at them to remove them. If left in they will rust and stain the canvas.

A number 13 or 14 sail needle will be about right for this job, and you should use good quality sail twine twisted for hand sewing. That made for machine sewing is twisted the opposite way, and tends to unlay as you sew with it. Cut off about two yards of it and thread it into the needle. Bring the two ends of the twine together (you will use it doubled) and wax it well with a piece of beeswax, then roll it across your thigh with the palm of your hand until the two strands are twisted together.

Grip the needle lightly between your thumb and forefinger, resting its eye in one of the dimples in your seaming palm. Push the point up through the doubled edge as shown in Figure 86c. Pull the twine through, but leave about two inches of the ends protruding. No knot is needed since your next stitch will tie one. Push the needle down through the single thickness of the cloth, back up through it, and then up through the doubled edge as shown in Figure 86c. Pull the twine through, making sure the loop catches the two-inch ends you have left. Pull the stitch tight. Take your next four or five stitches in the same manner, letting each of them catch the ends as it is drawn down.

You can now hook your bench hook into the seam and attach its lanyard to the bench on which you are sitting, a couple of feet to your right. This hook holds the material so that you have something to push against when you shove the needle through the canvas with the palm. For this reason, your thrust with the needle should be in line with the lanyard of the bench hook. Pull each stitch down as you go, but do not haul it too tight or you will pucker the cloth.

Your stitches should be about ¼ inch long for this work, and as evenly spaced as you can get them. If your stitching is going properly, the stitches should appear at right angles to the doubled edge, as shown in Figure 86d. This is easy to manage, once you get the hang of it, and while its only importance has to do with appearance, you might as well get it right. If you turn the cloth over, as in Figure 86e, the stitches on the back side of the seam will be seen to run diagonally.

Sew the tabling down all the way across the after end of the piece, moving the bench hook from time to time to bring the work back to a comfortable position. Take it slowly at first. You will gain speed as you practice, but don't gain it at the expense of evenly spaced stitches or equal tension. When you reach the end, pass the needle back under the last five or six stitches, draw the twine through, and cut off the end.

Now, with this experience behind us, we shall make the seam between the two pieces. Study Figure 87, which shows the way in which

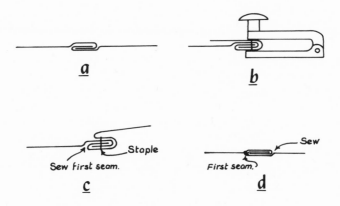

Fig. 87—Steps in making a flat seam.

the seam is folded into the canvas. If you make each fold one inch wide, the black pencil marks denoting the edge of the finished canvas will lie right over one another. Fold the pieces together as in Figure 87a, then fold the right side over again to the left and staple as shown in Figure 87b. Now fold the right side back where it was and turn the piece over.

You should now have one exposed doubled edge where the first seam is to be sewn, exactly as you sewed the tabling. When you have done this, you can remove the staples, since the stitches will hold the pieces in position. Turn the work over and sew the seam down on the other side in the same manner. Assemble the two pieces for the other dodger, and seam them together in the same way.

Now crease and staple a tabling all the way around both dodgers (you have already finished it on the after edge of the first dodger). If you have trouble at the corners where there will be six thicknesses, cut out some of the material from the corner, but do not remove more than is necessary. It is quite possible to sew six thicknesses, and it will flatten down when it is finished. Sew these tablings in just as you did the first one.

Now, decide where you want to attach the dodger. The upper edge can be lashed to the lifeline. The upper after corner should be lashed to a stanchion to enable you to stretch the dodger taut. The lower edge can be secured to pad eyes, through scuppers, or to any conveniently placed fastening of this sort. The forward end should attach to the side and top of the doghouse. I find that my headsail sheets come through under the dodgers very nicely. Mark the chosen points of attachment on the canvas. (See Figure 84.)

If you have a grommet set, you can place brass grommets at these marks to carry the lanyards. If not, make some worked grommets as described here. They will not corrode, are nice looking, and well worth knowing how to make. For these you will need some brass rings about ⅝ inch in diameter.

Draw a ⅞ inch circle on the tabling where the grommet is to be located. Make a hole in the center of this circle. Either shove a sharp pricker through the canvas, or punch out a ¼ inch hole with a leather punch. This looks awfully small, but it will stretch out as you work the grommet. Do not make it larger to begin with, or you will not have as strong a grommet as you should.

Fill a sail needle with twine, using four or five strands to make a nice fat yarn. Wax this and roll it. Pass the needle through the ¼-inch hole as shown in Figure 88b, bringing the point up through the cloth on the marked ⅞-inch outer circle. Haul the twine through, but leave a couple inches of the ends sticking out. Put the brass ring in place, and take another stitch just like the last one, again coming up through the cloth on the outer circle, and catch the ends of the twine under the stitch as you haul it down good and tight. Sew right around the circle, spacing your stitches about $\frac{3}{32}$ inch apart on the large marked circle, and hauling each stitch tight as you sew. When you have gone around the circle, the grommet should appear as in Figure 88d. It should be hard and stiff, and will take an enormous strain if properly made.

Eye-splice short lines or lanyards into these grommets (Figure 89), and whip the ends. Your dodgers are now ready to lash in place and

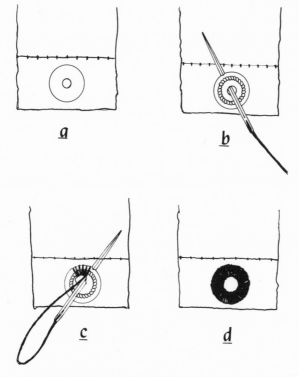

Fig. 88—*Making a "made" or sewn grommet.*

use. I have found a slipped rolling hitch to be ideal for attaching them to the lifelines and stanchions. This knot holds securely, yet it can be loosened in an instant, even when it is wet.

If you have enough canvas left over, you may wish to make an envelope-shaped bag in which to stow these dodgers when they are not in use. This should present no difficulty to you now, and it will keep the dodgers together and in their place. With these projects behind you, you will probably find a host of other canvas articles to make —things you have always wanted but never felt up to trying to make for yourself.

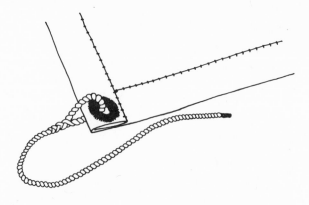

Fig. 89—Short line eye-spliced into a made grommet.

YOU *CAN* LEARN TO SPLICE WIRE

For many years I regarded wire splicing as a special mystery—the secret domain of the initiated few—although I had always enjoyed knot work and rope splicing. At one time I did endeavor to splice a new lifeline for a yacht, and, with the help of one of the standard books on the subject, managed to make an eyesplice that almost satisfied me. The fact that it looked as if it had been made by a seven year old child and took me all afternoon did, however, serve to reinforce my respect for professional riggers, as well as my conviction that wire splicing was beyond the ken of ordinary mortals. I felt I had no choice but to go on using swaged end-fittings.

I don't like swaged end-fittings. I have had too many of them break under way, and twice with results that were rather breath-taking, to say the least. I suppose they may be justified on a racing boat in order to be able to use the slightly smaller 1 x 19 wire, but I see no justification for them on a cruising boat. The sleeve-type fittings such as Nicopress and Telurit seem to be more reliable, but they too require a special and expensive tool and an assortment of the proper size sleeves. Then too, in spite of the manufacturers' assurance to the contrary, I am sure there is more likelihood of galvanic corrosion where these sleeves touch the stainless wire than is the case in a splice where there is only one metal throughout. Moreover, I know that a splice will not give way, and that it can be made at any time, ashore or afloat, with no special equipment, or facilities other than those always to be found on my boat.

Some time ago, a close inspection of my rigging revealed that it all had to be replaced. This in itself was not so much of a blow. I had long been dreaming of changing over from a sloop to a cutter rig. The cost of having the job done professionally, however, was a little more than the budget could bear. Joe Barnett's *Majoba* was lying alongside at the time, and Joe—a longtime friend of mine—offered to help me with the job. I jumped at the chance. The saving in labor costs would allow me to use stainless wire throughout, and I desperately wished to get away from the maintenance and replacement problems inherent in galvanized rigging.

Joe showed me a method of splicing which was quite new to me, and I was delighted to find that, after the first two or three splices I was able to turn out a very nice looking splice in a reasonable length of time. With Joe's help, the rigging job was completed quickly, and the finished result was doubly rewarding. In addition to the new rig, I acquired the realization that wire splicing need be no more formidable a task than rope work, and that anyone can learn to do it if he is shown a good method and taken step by step through the procedure a couple of times. I can assure you that there is a great deal of satisfaction to be had from the knowledge that you need never again postpone an improvement in your rigging because of the splicing involved, and that a coil of wire carried in your bilge means that you can always turn out a replacement shroud or stay on a moment's notice.

You need relatively few tools for wire splicing, but you may have to add one or two to those you already have for rope work. One of my favorite tools is an old screwdriver modified as shown in Figure 90.

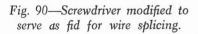 

Fig. 90—Screwdriver modified to serve as fid for wire splicing.

The blade should not be more than three inches long. The tip should be modified so that it becomes a sort of flattened-out spoon with a thin but rounded edge at the tip. This tool can be used to open the lay of a rope that stubbornly refuses to admit a fid or spike, and does so without nicking the wires in the process. Be sure to use a good quality screwdriver to make this tool, as the strands of a stainless wire rope are quite hard and will soon cut grooves in the edges of a tool that is not sufficiently hard.

To my knowledge, the second tool is not available commercially, but is quite simple to make. I made mine, and several for friends of mine, from *hard* stainless steel sheet about $\frac{1}{16}$ inch thick. The stainless must be hard, for the reason mentioned in connection with the screwdriver, and if you cannot find stainless that meets this requirement, tool steel will work quite well. I have found that a strip cut from the side of a worn-out plane iron works very well, since it can be hardened to the desired degree without making it brittle.

Cut a strip as shown in Figure 91b, one half inch wide at the tip and increasing to one inch over a length of six inches, then continuing one inch for an additional two inches. Don't worry about the rounded shape of the tip at this time. Scribe a centerline on the strip, and then, holding it in a bench vise (or a sheet metal brake, if you have access to one), bend the material along the centerline to give approximately the sections shown in the drawing. This fold should be not less than 90°, and can even be a definite U-shape if you find it easier.

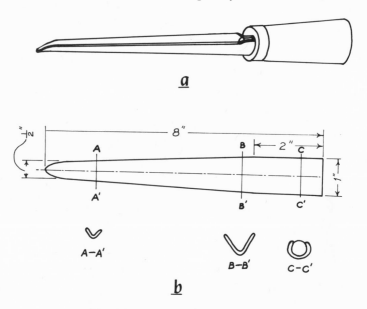

Fig. 91—Special wire-splicing fid.

Lay a two inch length of $\frac{5}{16}$ inch rod in the handle end of the fold and form the sheet metal around it to form a tang for the wooden handle. While it is not strictly necessary, it is a good idea to tack this rod in place with a welder. Make a wooden handle with a tightly fitting hole and drive it onto the tang you have just formed.

By holding the handle of the tool, you can now easily finish it down with a file. The edges should all be smoothed and rounded and the tip shaped as shown in Figure 91a. The very end of the tip should be quite thin so you can easily insert it under a strand of wire. In the following discussion, I'll refer to this tool simply as the "fid," although you will soon see how superior it is to an ordinary fid. The method of splicing to be described can be done with an ordinary fid, but this tool makes it and most other work with wire rope much easier.

You will also need access to a bench vise mounted on a good solid bench or table, and something with which to cut wire rope. This can be a pair of bolt-cutters, a hack saw with a fine-toothed blade, or a sharp cold chisel and something to serve as an anvil. A pair of diagonal or end-cutting pliers, a pair of vise-grip pliers, some electrician's tape or better still some ordinary adhesive tape with a cloth rather than plastic backing, and some small marline or heavy sail twine will complete your kit. An ordinary pair of slip-joint pliers will prove useful for hauling strands through tucks and for squeezing the splice to its final shape.

I see very little point in using anything but stainless wire for yacht rigging. Its higher initial cost is far more than offset by the fact that it is good for almost the life of the yacht, and if you do your own splicing, this increase in initial expense can be countered by the saving in end fittings and swaging. Spliced ends do mean, of course, that you cannot use 1 x 19 wire for standing rigging. Theoretically it can be spliced, but the results I have seen at the hands of professional riggers have not impressed me very favorably. Modern 6 x 7 or 7 x 7 wire splices easily, and is just as satisfactory for your shrouds and stays. The slight decrease in diameter possible with 1 x 19 wire may be significant for a candidate for the America's Cup, but means nothing at all on a cruising boat, nor, for that matter, on the average ocean racer.

When you do buy stainless wire, be sure that it is *preformed*. This means that the strands, before being laid up, have been given a helical twist so that they lie inert in the lay of the finished wire rope. It can be cut with no fuss, whereas stainless wire that is not preformed will unlay like an angry cobra when you cut it, and God help you if a seizing slips off the end.

For your practice splices, and I suggest that you make four or five of them, you will need about eight feet of ¼ inch wire. It might as well be galvanized for this purpose, and should be 6 x 7, since this is simpler to splice. If you wish to practice serving your splices, get some *good* tarred marline, or some seizing wire. I prefer four strand seizing wire, since it continues to hold even if one or two strands get chafed through or break for one reason or another. Of course, the seizing wire should be *dead soft*. Buy three or four thimbles to fit the wire.

About ten inches from the end of the 6 x 7 wire, put a good firm seizing. Unlay it back to this point and whip the ends of the strands. I usually just tape these ends with adhesive tape. Do not use more than two or three turns of tape or the strand will be difficult to tuck. Your wire should now look like Figure 92, the black central strand in the drawing representing the fibre core of the rope which you can cut off close up against the seizing at point A.

Seize a thimble to the wire as shown in Figure 93. It should be so

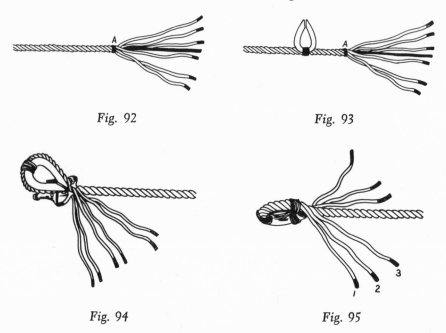

Fig. 92   Fig. 93

Fig. 94   Fig. 95

located that, when the rope is bent around it, the seizing at point A comes just to the end of the thimble. You can judge this well enough by eye, but try to get it as close as possible. Make this first seizing strong and tight, as it will have to take a fair amount of strain when you bend the wire around the thimble in the next step.

Now bend the rope tightly around the thimble and clamp it in place with the vise-grip pliers as shown in Figure 94. This takes a bit of juggling the first few times you try it, and you will find that the adjustment of the vise-grips is quite critical. If they are properly adjusted, you can grasp the wire with them well up on the thimble and when you close them they will stretch the wire tightly around the thimble and clamp it securely together at the throat. Don't get discouraged if you have a little trouble with this step at first—it becomes quite simple once you get the hang of it. This is one place, however, where you may welcome a second pair of hands during your early experiments. With the vise-grip pliers holding the wire around the thimble, clap on two more seizings as shown in Figure 95. These should be hauled good and tight, and should be down as far on the legs of the thimble as you can get them. In fact, I often use a racking seizing here, working back and forth between the two legs of the thimble. Remove the vise-grips and your work should look like Figure 95.

Purely for the sake of avoiding confusion in the steps that are to follow, I shall coin a few terms and define them at this point. They are quite without precedent, and their only value lies in making a lucid explanation possible. Please don't be upset if you disagree with my choice of terms—any others would have done as well. The strands of the wire rope beyond the thimble—the ten inch ones which you have unlaid and whipped—I shall call *end strands*. The strands of the longer portion of the rope on the other side of the thimble, I shall call *cable strands*. The advantages of this arbitrary distinction will become apparent, I think, as we go along.

With the eye of the splice to your left, as in Figure 95, look at the end strands as they leave the seizing at point A. Select the three of them that naturally lead across the top of the splice, viewed in this position, and arange them as shown in Figure 95. Make some small tabs from adhesive tape and numer these tabs 1, 2, and 3 with a ball-point pen. Stick these numbered tabs on the strands to identify them. Notice that strand number 1 lies to your left as it comes out of the

Fig. 96

Fig. 97

seizing, strand number 2 is just to the right of it, and strand number 3 is to the right of number 2.

Tuck the other three strands under the splice to keep them out of the way and put a temporary seizing around them to hold them until we need them. Hold strands 1, 2, and 3 to one side for a moment so you can see the cable strands where the first tucks are to be made. With the modified screwdriver, lift three strands as shown in Figure 96. The screwdriver should pass *over* the fibre core of the rope. It may take a little effort to get the screwdriver to enter the rope, but once you have raised the first cable strand, the rest will be easy. Selecting just the right place to make this first opening is a knack that you will only gain by practice, and its proper location makes a lot of difference in the appearance of the finished splice. Looking down on the splice, as in Figure 96, insert the tool in such a place that, after passing under three strands and emerging on the other side of the rope, its blade will be approximately horizontal. In each of your practice splices, vary this location a little and notice the effect this has on the throat of the finished splice. You will soon learn where to open the lay. It should be done as near as possible to the thimble, still allowing the tool to pass under three cable strands in a horizontal plane.

With the strands open, you can insert the fid you have made. The farther you shove it through the opening, the farther its wedge shape will open the strands. With the fid in place, tuck end strand number 1 by passing it through the channel in the fid in the direction shown in Figure 96. Notice that this end strand passes under *three* cable strands in this first tuck. Remove the fid and haul the tucked strand as tight as you can, pulling it well back against the thimble but taking care not to kink it as you pull it through.

Insert the fid again *in the same place,* but this time pass it under only two cable strands. This time you will not need to use the screw driver to open the lay of the rope. With the fid in place, tuck end strand number 2 as shown in Figure 97, and haul it up as tightly as you can.

Insert the fid again *in the same place,* lifting only one cable strand this time, and tuck end strand number 3 as shown in Figure 98. Withdraw the fid and haul the tucked strands up tightly against the thimble. This completes the first phase of the splice, and your work should now look like Figure 99. The three tucked end strands should come out through three adjacent spaces as shown in the drawing.

Turn the splice around so the eye is to your left, and it should look like Figure 100. Now cut the seizing holding the three untucked strands together and prepare three more number tabs from adhesive tape, numbering these tabs 4, 5, and 6. Take a look at the way in which these remaining three strands emerge from the seizing at the thimble. Stick the number 4 adhesive label on the strand which comes

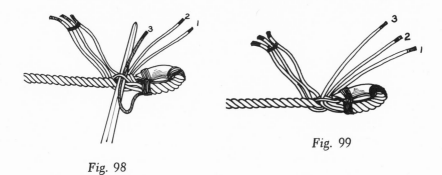

Fig. 98

Fig. 99

out next to end strand 3. Of the remaining strands, this should lie closest to the thimble, or to your left as you view the splice in Figure 100. Strand number 5 lies just to the right of 4, and strand number 6 is at the extreme right. Label all these. You can dispense with this labelling after you have made three or four splices, but it is a big help in the beginning.

Hold the splice on the bench with the eye to your left as shown in Figure 101. The already-tucked strands 1, 2, and 3 should be emerging from the side nearest you, and will probably be pointing downward

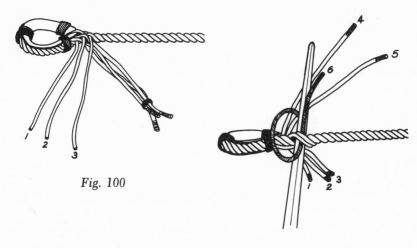

Fig. 100

Fig. 101

toward the floor. Insert the fid *in the same space entered by the first three strands, but pointing in the opposite direction*—in other words, away from you. Pass it over the fibre core but under only two of the cable strands this time. Tuck end strand 6 under these two cable strands as shown in Figure 101, sticking the strand through away from you in the same direction in which you have just inserted the fid. Withdraw the fid and haul strand 6 tight. Take care as you do this to avoid kinking strand 6. With a little careful maneuvering, you can

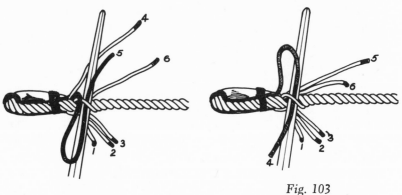

Fig. 102

Fig. 103

get it to slide through without deforming it, and this will make succeeding steps easier and the finished splice better looking. Insert the fid in the same place, raising only one cable strand this time, and tuck end strand number 5 under it, as shown in Figure 102. This strand should be tucked away from you, in the same direction as strand number 6. You are now left with only one strand to tuck—number 4. This last tuck is the "locking tuck," and holds the preceding ones in place. Lift the cable strand under which you have just

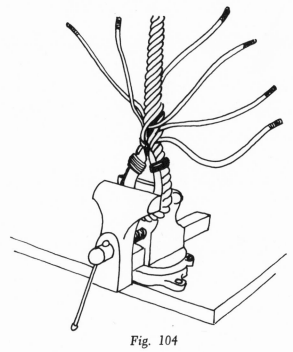

Fig. 104

tucked end strand number 5, and open the space with the fid. Tuck end strand 4 under this same cable strand, *but in the opposite direction,* as shown in Figure 103. Remove the fid and pull all six of the tucked strands down tight.

As you examine what you have done so far, you should see an end strand emerging from each space between the cable strands. No space should be empty, and none should have more than one end strand

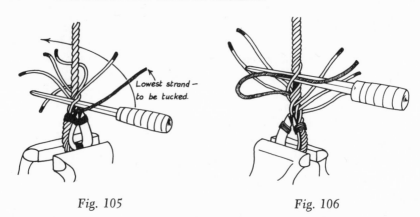

Fig. 105   Fig. 106

emerging from it. Some of these emerging end strands will be con-siderably farther from the thimble than will others. Select the end strand emerging *nearest the thimble* for the first tuck of the second tier.

Place the eye in the bench vise, as shown in Figure 104, with this lowest strand coming out on the side toward you where you can see it and get at it. With the fid in your right hand, lift the cable strand which lies to the *left* of this lowest end strand. Shove the fid through from right to left, as shown in Figure 105.

Now push the handle of the fid *away* from you, letting it swing around behind the rope with the rope as a fulcrum. In doing this, it will "screw" itself up along the lay of the rope. At some point, usu-ally about 120° around from your starting position, you will feel the resistance to the fid suddenly give way. At this point, the cable strand you have been lifting frees itself from the lay of the rope and lifts above it, or out away from it if you prefer. This is the correct place to tuck the end strand, and your fid will locate it for you if you give it a chance. Don't worry if this appears to be a long way from the thimble. As I have said, the fid will have rotated through about 120° (anticlockwise as you look down at it), and in doing so it will have "screwed" itself some distance up the lay of the rope, but this *is* the correct place for the next tuck.

Take the lowest emerging end strand—the one which comes out just to the right of the cable strand you now have lifted on the fid. Bring this end strand to the left, over the lifted cable strand, and tuck it under from left to right as shown in Figure 106. As you pull it through, you will notice that there is a point at which its snaky shape makes it lie comfortably in place spiralling around the cable strand. Do not draw it tighter than this. This shape of the preformed strands will tell you just where they should lie after each tuck. Notice too, that in tucking this end strand you have simply *wound it round* the cable strand.

Now insert the fid from right to left under the cable strand which lies immediately to the left of the one you have just lifted and worked on. Rotate the fid around to the back of the splice as before, stopping when you feel the resistance give way as the strand lifts out of the lay. As you do this, notice that the fid rides around on the previously tucked strand and rolls it neatly back into the lay of the rope. This is why we shall proceed from here on in a spiral fashion, tucking each successive strand as we proceed clockwise (looking down) around the rope. Now, with this cable strand raised, tuck under it the end strand which emerges immediately to its right just as you did before. Bring the end strand over to the left, and through under the cable strand from left to right. Pull the end strand through until it lies naturally in the lay of the rope.

Work your way around the rope in this fashion, a strand at a time, until you have tucked each end strand three times. Theoretically, you should reduce each end strand by half after the second tuck, but I have found that I get a very nice looking splice without bothering about this additional and time consuming procedure. You will have to turn the splice in the vise from time to time in order to have convenient access to the strand you are working on.

When you have finished the three tiers of tucks, the end strands will be emerging at different heights along the splice and sticking out in different directions. This is as it should be. With an ordinary pair of slip-joint pliers, squeeze the splice to shape beginning near the thimble and working around in a spiral fashion with the lay of the rope until you reach the end of the splice. As you do this, the splice will smooth out and adjust itself. If, in the course of this, you work some excess slack down toward the ends of some of the tucked strands, pull on them with the pliers to take out this slack.

When the splice is relatively even and uniform, you will see that it has actually become a six-strand rope, with each of its strands consisting of one original end strand wound spirally around one original cable strand. This method of tucking is termed "Liverpool fashion,"

Fig. 107

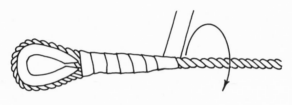

Fig. 108

as distinguished from the over-and-under tucks used in a sailor's rope splice. Although some authorities advocate tucking over and under with wire rope as well, I much prefer tucking Liverpool fashion. It produces a splice which looks better and is much easier to make, especially with larger sizes of wire where the sheer stiffness of the strands becomes a problem in itself. It also avoids sharp kinks in the strands which are unavoidable in over-and-under tucking, and which become the natural places for the splice to break under heavy loads.

Cut off the emerging strands with your diagonal or end cutters, as close to the rope as you can without letting the last tucks slip out. Your splice should now look like Figure 107. Tape the splice, as shown in Figure 108, using adhesive or electrician's friction tape. Work the cut ends of the strands in as you tape over them so they lie as flat as possible under the tape. Note that the tape parcelling is wound on *with* the lay of the rope. Pull it as tight as you can and make a nice smooth job of it.

Start your marline service by making a few turns over the free end of the marline. This will hold it firmly in place without the use of knots. When serving with seizing wire, secure the end by opening the lay of the rope with the screw driver and tucking the end under a couple of strands. Then bend it back and serve over it for a few turns.

You really should use a serving mallet to do a first class job, but I have found that it is possible to get acceptable results by hand with both wire and marline. Haul each turn as tight as you can get it and then have a helper hold it against slipping while you get ready for the next turn. Wrap the last few turns over a marlinespike, as shown in Figure 109. This will hold these turns up off the splice far enough to enable you to pass the end of the marline or wire back under them as shown in the drawing. Remove the spike, and pull these turns tight, one at a time; then pull the excess through and cut off the end as close as possible.

Beat the splice with a mallet, turning it as you do so. It will take a nice symmetrical shape, and should end up looking something like Figure 110. Make four or five of these practice splices before you attempt anything you care about. You will learn a great deal in the course of this. Don't be afraid to experiment with such things as the location of the opening for the first tuck. This is the only way to understand what a slight variation in this location will do to the finished splice. When you do begin splicing your own rigging, start with running rigging such as a halyard. The flexible wire, such as 6 x 19, used for this is very easy to work with, and you can become familiar with the technique and with the anatomy of a proper splice before you encounter the additional mechanical problems of dealing with stiffer strands.

Keep a few basic principles in mind. Do everything you can to

Fig. 109

Fig. 110

avoid kinking or nicking the end strands as you tuck them or the cable strands as you lift them. A kinked strand will cause trouble in the remainder of the splice, and a nicked strand is very likely to break at some later date. Try to preserve the original "kinky" shape of the end strands. This shape makes them more capable of finding their own natural position in the lay of the splice as you make the tucks. Try to get about the same amount of tension on all the end strands as you make the tucks. This is most important during the second tier of tucks. Of course, the splice will "pull in" and even itself up under load, but it is well to have the initial tension in the tucks as uniform as possible.

You may wish, at some time, to use 7 x 7 wire for standing rigging. It is just like 6 x 7, except that it has a wire core rather than a fibre one. The usual practice of fishermen, and many riggers as well, is to cut this core out before making the splice, just as we have done with the fibre core in the 6 x 7 wire. This defeats the whole purpose of using 7 x 7 wire, and is a ridiculous and reprehensible practice. You might as well start with 6 x 7 wire, since you have lost the additional strength of the seventh strand. 7 x 7 wire can be spliced just as we have spliced the 6 x 7, with one difference which I shall now describe.

After you have made the first tuck with end strand number 2, as in Figure 97, and before you withdraw the fid, tuck the wire core through alongside it. You can always identify the core because it is perfectly straight without the spiral kinks characteristic of the six other strands. After you have pulled these two strands through (number 2 and the core), wind the core up along the cable strand for three tucks before continuing with the rest of the first tier of tucks. Then finish off the splice just as you did with the 6 x 7 wire.

When you are working your way around making the second and third tiers of tucks, each time you come to the cable strand around which the core is tucked, be sure you tuck your end strand *under the cable strand only,* and not under the core. All the rest of the splice is made in the same way and you have preserved the strength of the original 7 x 7 wire. Even if you should farm out some of your future rigging to a rigger, specify that the core is not to be cut out of splices in 7 x 7 wire. Then, if you expect this to be carried out, you had better plan to be there when the splices are made. One just can't tell, once the splices have been served over.

In the course of this wire splicing, you are likely to get scratched up a bit from the ends of the strands. I don't know how to avoid this and it annoys me. After rigging my yacht, I looked as if I had been involved in a cat fight. At the same time, I have found a great deal of satisfaction in mastering a procedure which I used to be afraid to try. I also take a great deal of pride in my rigging, and in the fact that I did it myself. I know that now I can do a first class splice in about an hour's time. I know every splice on the yacht, and that I can trust them to hold. I also know I saved a lot of money. I hope you try wire splicing yourself. It isn't the easiest skill to learn, but it's nowhere near as difficult as I had thought, and it gives one a great sense of independence as well as accomplishment once it is mastered.

IX
THE DINGHY

A LIFTING HOOK FOR THE DINGHY

We use our dinghy a great deal, since we like unpopulated coves and anchorages, and we often prefer riding at anchor to the noise and confusion of a yacht harbor. This means we have to get the dinghy aboard and put it into the water frequently, and often when there are just the two of us to handle it. Getting it over the side or back on deck is not so much of a problem, but handling it beneath the main boom and over a skylight can be very tricky, especially if the yacht is rolling. This problem is aggravated if the stowing space for the dinghy is cramped and it must be lowered carefully into just the right position in its chocks.

I have a snap shackle in the end of the dinghy's stern line. This is snapped into a ring at the bow to form a lifting bridle. In the center of this bridle, I have spliced a hard eye. The halyard is snapped into this eye, and the dinghy is lifted out of the water, over the lifelines, and onto the side deck, where we lower it *on its beam ends* with the bottom toward the rail. The lifting hook, shown in Figure 111, is then

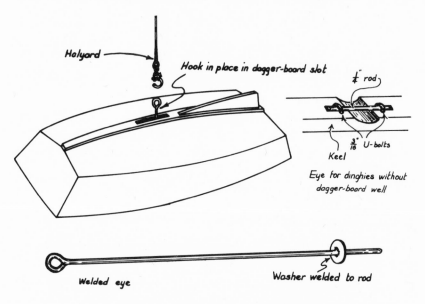

Fig. 111—Lifting hook for dinghy.

shoved down through the dagger-board slot until the eye protrudes at the bottom. The halyard is now shifted to this eye.

Now, when I take up on the halyard, the dinghy is lifted upside down and my wife can easily guide it into place over the skylight and hold it there while I lower it into its chocks. Reversing the drill, of course, gets it off the deck and into the water.

If your dinghy has no dagger-board well, the same routine can be followed by setting a lifting eye into the keel or skeg at the point of balance. The eye shown in Figure 111 works well, and does not protrude enough to be damaged if the dinghy is beached or set down on a concrete quay. The ¼ inch rod should be long enough to extend well beyond the transverse notch on either end. If it is carefully bedded into the groove, it acts as a splint to compensate for the wood removed. The U-bolts should be set up firmly with flat washers, spring washers and nuts, and then cut off. Smooth their ends with a file to protect bare feet, and paint the ends unless they are bronze or stainless.

CHAIN GUARD FOR THE DINGHY RAIL

It is often necessary to use the dinghy to lay out the kedge, or to clear and lift a fouled anchor, and this should be kept in mind when the dinghy is being selected. It should be very hard in the bilges so as to afford a good stable working platform. Too tender a boat is useless for this kind of work.

Paying out or taking in chain over the dinghy's rail is certain to damage the paint or varnish, and usually chews up the wooden rail as well. The portable fairlead shown here (Figure 112) will protect your rails as well as making it much easier to haul in heavy chain. It can be clamped in place anywhere along the gunwale, on the outboard motor mount at the stern, or on the bow transom in the case of a pram.

It is best made from stainless steel, since this will eliminate the rust problem as well as providing a hard enough surface to let the chain slide easily. The saddle portion over which the chain passes should be made from sheetstock of about 16 gauge, and the forming of this is tricky at best. Take it to a good sheet metal worker to be made. The curvature of this piece should be fairly regular and of at least a seven inch radius to make it easy to haul in chain over it. The clamps and

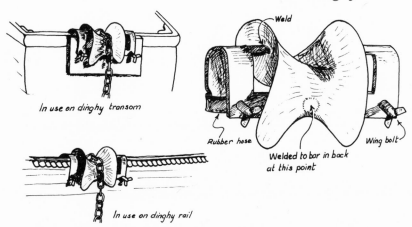

Fig. 112—Chain "guard" or fairlead to protect rail of dinghy.

frame can be made of ³⁄₁₆ inch bar stock and welded to the saddle. No special effort need be made to polish the piece—it will increase the cost but not the utility. Slide a couple of pieces of rubber hose on the jaws of the clamps as shown in the sketch to keep them from slipping.

If the stainless steel work discourages you too much, the wooden version shown in Figure 113, works just as well. Make the bar of oak, and have the clamps made from steel, preferably stainless. The saddle portion is first glued up around the bar out of strips of a dense wood such as live oak. When the glue is dry, the saddle shape may be

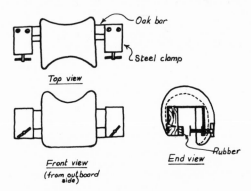

Fig. 113—Alternate design for chain fairlead to be made from hard wood.

carved out using chisels and wood rasps and finishing with sandpaper. Do not thin out the wood too much in the center portion of the saddle, as this is where the chain will ride and it will have to carry quite a load as well as being subject to wear from the chain.

Prime and paint the wooden portion of this fairlead, except for the surface of the saddle across which the chain will ride. To finish this, warm the surface of the wood for a few minutes in a low oven or in front of an open fire, and then rub tallow into the wood. The wood should be just hot enough to melt the grease and absorb it. Load it up with all the tallow it will absorb, since this will make the chain slide easily, especially when it is wet.

Keep the fairlead stowed in a plastic bag to keep the tallow off other items of your gear, and give it a good greasing two or three times a year. The small amount of time this requires is nothing compared to refinishing or replacing the rails on your dinghy.

DINGHY OARLOCKS

Because of the limitations on size and weight, the average cruising yacht's dinghy is a compromise at best. Unfortunately, its usefulness is often diminished still further by oarlocks which are totally inadequate. Those shown here are expensive to have made, but look what you get for your money. It is impossible to lose them, unless you lose the oars too. In even the roughest going, the oar cannot jump out of the oarlock, yet you have complete freedom of motion. You can let go of the oars and let them trail in the water, and this is worth a lot when you are laying out an anchor on a windy day, since they are always in position for a quick stroke or two to hold your own against the wind.

Start with a good pair of oars, and sand and finish them to suit. I like to paint the blades a bright yellow, as they can then be much more easily seen if they ever go adrift. Give the rest of the oars several coats of a good varnish. Incidentally, I like to shape the handles so they are oval in cross section rather than round, then I can tell by the feel of them, even in the dark, what position the blades are in relative to the water.

The loom should be leathered at the proper pivot point for a distance of seven or eight inches. Glue the leather on after sanding the varnish in the area and fasten it at the seam with small copper tacks or nails with their heads sunk into the leather. Use as few tacks as possible, as they do weaken the oar.

Now have the oarlocks made of stainless steel. The tube should be a loose fit over the leather, and should have walls about $\frac{1}{16}$ inch thick. The yoke portion can be cut from sheet stock and should be a little heavier in gauge. Drill holes for the pivot pins. Turn these pins out of stainless steel rod stock with a little shoulder as shown in Figure 114, to position them positively in the holes and to provide a larger area for the weld. They should be welded securely, all around the shoulder. Be sure that the pins do not project into the inside of the tube—everything inside should be clear and smooth.

The yoke portion, with the pin holes drilled, is now formed to wrap around the tube and closed to its final shape over the pivot pins. These are peened enough to form heads, and finished smooth. The pins for the oarlock sockets are made from rod stock of the appropriate diameter, and welded to the yokes.

The collar, made from leather strip, should now be placed on the

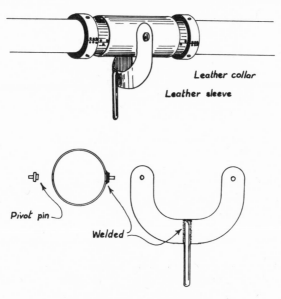

Leather collar

Leather sleeve

Pivot pin

Welded

Fig. 114—Dinghy oarlocks.

blade end of the leather sleeve. Coat the strip with glue, tack one end in place, and then roll it on tightly until you have built up a collar about ⅜ inch thick. Tack the end of the strip in place and cut off the surplus.

Now wrap a couple of layers of masking tape around the other end of the leather sleeve where the other collar will be placed, and then thoroughly grease the exposed leather with tallow. The tape will keep the tallow off the portion where you will want the glue to take.

Slide the completed oarlock over the handle of the oar and down against the leather collar. Remove the masking tape, and glue the second collar in place, and the job is finished. Once or twice a season, work a little grease into the leather sleeve under the tube to protect the leather and to allow the oar to turn freely.

One word of caution. If you make a pair of these, paint your name on the blades of the oars. They will be the envy of every yachtsman in your harbor.

FENDER CUSHIONS FOR THE DINGHY

Really adequate fenders for a dinghy have always been a problem. The usual rope fender around the gunwale usually fails to give protection to the sloping topsides of a yacht with an overhanging stern. It also fails to protect the dinghy's own topsides if it is tied up alongside a low concrete wall, or used to land on a rocky shore. The miniature editions of conventional yacht fenders are all but useless, since they always hang too low to protect the dinghy and are too light in weight to stay in position.

The cushion shown here is a perfectly satisfactory cushion in its own right, either for use on deck or in the dinghy itself. Filled with kapok or closed cell foam, it provides useful flotation gear. In addition, it serves as a really effective fender for the dinghy when draped over the gunwale as shown in Figure 115. It offers a large, well padded surface on the outboard side, and its heavy plastic cover is exceptionally resistant to chafe.

If you decide to use kapok filling, make the cover first and then stuff it with the kapok. If you prefer a foam filling, and it is simpler, cut the foam to size and make the cover to fit it. Be sure you get *closed cell foam*. It is buoyant and will not soak up water. If you are

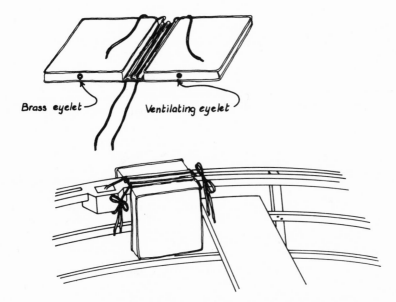

Brass eyelet

Ventilating eyelet

Fig. 115—Combination cushion and dinghy fender.

in doubt, test a small sample by trying to use it as a sponge in water. The closed cell type floats on top of the water and doggedly resists your attempts to get it to absorb water, while the open cell foam acts like a kitchen sponge.

Cut the foam to size—two pieces 12 inches square and 2 inches thick are about right. I have some knife-edge blades for my sabre saw, and these work very well for cutting foam. A bread knife with a wavy edge will also do a good job.

Lay out the patterns for the covers (or get your wife to do it), allowing about three inches gap between the two foam cushions as shown in Figure 115, for the "hinge" portion. If you want to do a very nice job, make up some piping by sewing strips of the plastic covering material around some ⅛ inch nylon cord. These can be sewn into the seams and give a very professional and finished look to the cushion.

Be sure to get a good heavy grade of plastic upholstery material for the covers, and make certain it is backed with fabric so you can sew it on a sewing machine. I'll plump for a bright yellow color which can be seen from a great distance.

Cut three or four 11-inch lengths of ½-inch diameter nylon rope, whip the ends, and lay them into the hinged portions between the two foam cushions. Sew between these lengths of rope so that each lies in its own pocket, so to speak. These will serve as a fender over the actual rail of the dinghy, as well as allowing the cushion to bend easily at this point. Sew a heavy nylon shoe string into each end of this hinge section to use to tie the fender in place on the dinghy.

Set a ventilator into each cushion cover. These are extremely important, since without them the cushion will be likely to explode if one of your larger guests sits on it suddenly. The ventilators may be either the small screened eyelets sold for this purpose, or ordinary brass grommets with a ⅜ inch opening.

Laid flat the cushions are just about right in size for a dinghy thwart, or may be used in the yacht cockpit. Draped over the dinghy gunwale and secured by the shoestring lanyards, they protect both your dinghy and the neighbor's yacht when you go aboard. Since one has to carry both deck cushions and dinghy fenders, why not make these combinations and save space.

If you don't care to make these from scratch, you can always achieve the same end by buying two approved flotation cushions, and having an upholsterer join them as shown in the drawings.

EMERGENCY KIT FOR THE DINGHY

If you use your dinghy much to explore the coves in which your yacht is anchored, a small permanently stowed emergency kit can be very welcome at times. After having gotten into a wide variety of difficulties from time to time, I have finally settled on the following items as sufficient to get me out of most of them:

1 combination wrench (supplied with my outboard and fitting almost everything on it).
1 pair of slip-joint pliers
1 spare spark plug for the outboard
1 small screw driver
1 ball of marline
1 knife

These items are wrapped in a couple of clean dry rags, and then the packet is placed in a tough plastic bag. The mouth of the bag is rolled several times to make a water tight closure, and fastened with two clothes pins. The bag is then stowed in a box made of thin tough wood.

Before you stow the spark plug, be sure to set the gap correctly for your outboard. This makes a great difference in the ease with which the motor will start, and is a lot easier to do at home or aboard the yacht than when you are trying to get the motor started while adrift in the dinghy.

Now, why this particular selection of items? There are just a certain number of things that can go wrong and which have to be dealt with before you can come back to the yacht. Probably the most common one is an outboard that stops and refuses to start. If you are not out of fuel, the chances are ten to one that the trouble is in the spark plug. Take it out and dry it off well with the rag in the kit. Also dry off the high tension lead to the spark plug while you are at it. See if the gap in the plug is fouled, and if so clean it out and dry it. Replace the plug and try the outboard again. If it doesn't go, remove the spark plug and replace it with the new one from the kit. If the motor still refuses to start, get out the oars.

Now, oars can break, and dinghy oars often have such small looms and are made from such soft wood that they are particularly prone to this. I broke one once while pulling back to the yacht into a wind that had sprung up after I had rowed three-quarters of a mile from the yacht. I tried sculling, as I had an oarlock on the transom of the dinghy especially for this, but I couldn't make any headway into the wind. I saw a sardine box floating by, and hauled it aboard. By splitting the slats of the box with my knife, I soon had six splints about a foot long. The broken ends of the oar fitted back together easily, and by binding the splints around the break with marline, I ended up with a strange-looking but perfectly serviceable oar, and quite quickly. Hence the marline and the wooden box for the kit. Now I don't have to depend on rescuing a floating fish box.

I have also lost oarlocks and had the sockets pull loose from the gunwale. With the screwdriver, you can reattach the sockets, inserting some splinters of wood into the screw holes if the screws will not hold. Even if you should loose the oarlock entirely, or break it, you can jury-rig one with the marline. Take several loose turns through the oar-lock socket or around the clamp if the dinghy is of open construction, and tie the ends together. Stick the oar through this marline loop, and you will find you can row quite effectively with it. Not as well as with an oarlock, but you can make it home.

Why the pliers? I don't know—perhaps I just like pliers. Anyway, I always seem to be finding uses for them. The kit can be clipped or lashed under one of the thwarts or in any secure and out of the way place in the dinghy. I'm willing to bet, though, that it doesn't stay there too long without being used.

EXTENSION STEERING HANDLE FOR THE OUTBOARD

If one sits in the stern of the average small dinghy, where he can reach the controls of the outboard motor, the bow rears out of the water to an alarming degree. This greatly reduces speed, makes the boat difficult to handle, and can be quite dangerous in choppy water or a high wind. The dinghy will trim much better and perform very much better if one sits on the center thwart. Unfortunately, one can-not reach the outboard controls from the center thwart.

The obvious answer is an extension for the steering handle which will allow one to sit farther forward and still operate the motor. Many years ago the manufacturers of an English outboard must have had someone in their employ who was able to grasp this fact, because they have sold extension handles for their motors for a long time. This engineering triumph is essentially a piece of broomstick which one jams in the motor's tiller, and it does enable one to steer from a forward position. Unfortunately, steering is only one part of controlling an outboard motor, and the gymnastics involved in the use of this par-ticular commercially made handle are even more frightening than sit-ting in the stern and letting the bow rise out of the water. One is more or less constantly leaping back and forth in the dinghy to adjust the throttle.

Having decided that I was a little too old to stand such a workout, I designed and made an extension handle which allows me to control the throttle as well as to steer the boat, and the design and construc-tion will be described here for the benefit of other less athletic yachtsmen. My extension was designed for the British Seagull motor, but with only slight modifications it can be equally effective for almost any of the more modern outboards.

The rubber grip is removed from the steering handle of the outboard, and the outside diameter of the handle is carefully measured. Buy a length of stainless steel or brass tubing of a size that will just slide easily over the steering handle—a piece ten inches long will be enough. At the same time get five or six inches of rod stock. I suggest ³⁄₁₆ inch diameter if you are using stainless steel and ¼ inch diameter if it is to be of brass.

Bend the throttle control fork from the rod stock, being careful to make the gap just the right width for an easy fit over the throttle lever. For a Seagull, make this gap exactly ⁵⁄₁₆ inch wide. Bend the fork to a slight curve as shown in Figure 116, and weld or braze it to the tubing as shown in the drawing.

Fit a piece of wooden dowel into the other end of the tubing. My first tendency was to make these handles too short for real comfort, so I suggest you make it too long to begin with and cut off a little at a time until it is just the right length for your boat. Sand the dowel, serve the end for a good grip, and finish off the serving with a Turkshead on each end of the serving. Enamel or varnish the completed handle, and it is ready for use.

Called the Borland Steering Extension, this handle is now available commercially at a very reasonable price, should you not wish to make it yourself. It is manufactured by Watermota, Ltd., Abbotskerwell, Newton Abbot, South Devon, England. Any British chandler who does not stock it can easily order it for you, and American chandlers can order it from any importer of British yacht gear.

Slide it over the motor's steering handle so that the fork engages the throttle control lever (Figure 117). Rotating the extension handle will now operate the throttle and you have complete control of the motor with no acrobatics at all. If you have a passenger who can sit forward, the handle can be slipped off in a moment and the motor operated as usual since the controls have not been altered in any way.

With this handle you may stand up in your dinghy and still control the motor as well as the steering. This can be a great help when checking the set of an anchor or having a look at a new anchorage, since one can always see down into the water better from a standing position.

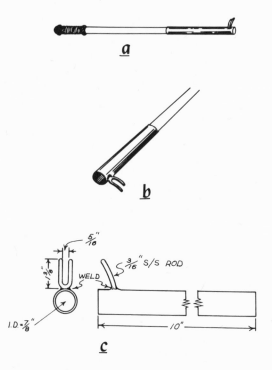

Fig. 116—*Steering extension: (a) completed handle; (b) tubing with throttle-control fork; (c) dimensions for Seagull handle.*

HANDY "ONE SHOT" CONTAINERS FOR OUTBOARD FUEL

An outboard motor for the dinghy is a very convenient thing to have aboard a cruising boat, but it must be small and light in weight to be practical. This usually means that its fuel tank is very small, so one is compelled to carry some spare fuel in the dinghy and to expect to have to fill the tank occasionally while under way.

In even the slightest chop, pouring fuel from a can into the fuel tank becomes an almost hopeless job, with a large part of the fuel going overboard or, worse yet, into the dinghy. We have found an almost ideal solution in quart size plastic "squeeze bottles" with mouths small

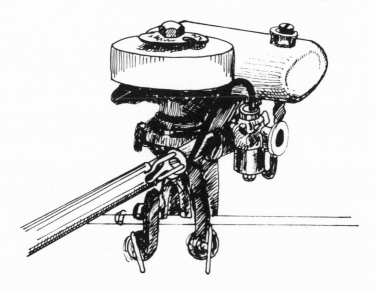

Fig. 117—Extension in place on a Seagull outboard. Note how fork engages throttle control.

enough to be easily inserted into the filler opening. Our little motor's tank is not quite filled by one of these bottles, so we never need worry about the tank overflowing while it is being filled. We just run it dry, and then we know it will hold more than the contents of one of the bottles.

The cap is removed, the neck of the bottle is quickly inserted into the filler opening, and the bottle is squeezed until it is empty. A rack for four of these bottles with a length of shock-cord to hold them in place, can usually be fitted to the underside of a thwart or in some other unused space in the dinghy, and will provide a reserve supply of fuel, always at hand and with no need for the always missing funnel.

X
NAVIGATION

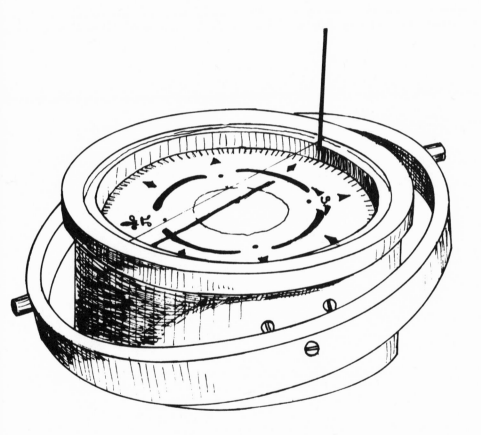

HOLDER FOR THE STOP WATCH

To be of maximum usefulness aboard a yacht, a stop watch should always be available, easy to get at, and easy to replace in its holder. As simple as this little design is, it answers these demands perfectly, and has been one of the most useful and satisfactory additions made to our yacht. From this rack, which is screwed to a bulkhead near the companionway, the watch can be lifted instantly, even in the dark, and can be replaced just as easily. The watch can be started and stopped while it is in place in the holder, if one is waiting for a radio time check. Perhaps most important of all, it doesn't disappear into the helmsman's pocket after he has used it to time a light—it goes back into the holder where it belongs, and where the next person on watch can find it.

The blocks were cut from teak to match the bulkhead, and beveled as shown (Figure 118). The corners were nicely rounded, and the blocks sanded and varnished. Screw holes were drilled and countersunk, and one of the blocks was screwed to place on the bulkhead. The watch

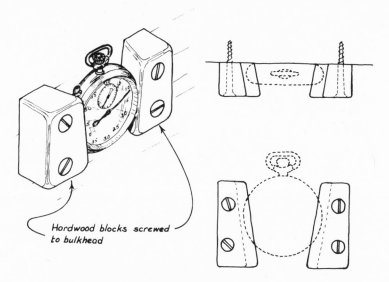

Fig. 118—*Holder for stop watch.*

was then held in place while the other block was located so the watch would jam in place at the right height. The holes for the screws were marked and drilled, and the second block was mounted.

Tucked into this little holder, my stopwatch has ridden out some rather violent weather with never a tendency to fall or to be shaken out. I suppose if we were ever thrown over far enough it might fall out, but so would everything else, for that matter.

WEATHERPROOF ROUGH LOG

On long cruises I find a rough log kept in the cockpit is a big help in obtaining an accurate and complete finished log. Without it, especially on night watches and in bad weather, there is a tendency for the helmsman to wait until he has been relieved and then try to write up the log from memory. Needless to say, many things are forgotten, and many of the entries are really just best-guesses.

I tried keeping a rough log in the cockpit before I stumbled onto this trick, but it was never successful. It always ended up crumpled, watersoaked, and often as not blown away. This one will stay put, is virtually indestructible, and can be written on equally well wet or dry.

It is made from a piece of marine plywood, ⅜ inch or ½ inch thick, and of a size to suit you. Mine is 8 inches x 11 inches, and I find it quite satisfactory. Cut the plywood to size and cement a sheet of white *matte* surface Formica on each side with one of the contact cements sold for this purpose. Follow the directions for the use of the cement carefully, and either clamp the pieces overnight or pound them exceedingly well with a mallet to insure a perfect bond along the edges.

Round the corners of the board and sand the edges smooth. Drill a hole through the top center to hang it by. Take apart an ordinary spring type clothespin. Fasten the half with the spring attached to the top of the log with a couple of tiny brass screws or copper nails, being sure to drill adequate holes for these through the Formica surface. Attach a lead pencil to the hole in the board by a length of cord. The pencil will stow in the clothespin when it is not in use. Varnish the clothespin and the plywood edges. Don't neglect to finish the inside of the hole. If you can keep water out of the edges of the plywood, it should never delaminate. (See Figure 119.)

You will find you can write easily on this, even when it is wet, and

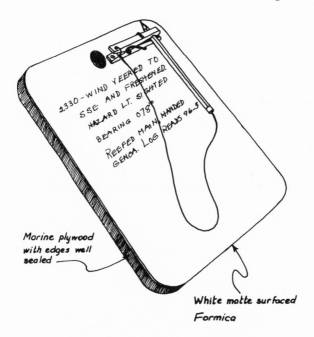

Marine plywood
with edges well
sealed

White matte surfaced
Formica

Fig. 119—Weatherproof rough log.

that the writing stays very well. It can be removed by scrubbing with scouring powder. If the surface loses its matte finish, go over it with a piece of very fine abrasive paper, used wet.

THE VERTICAL DANGER ANGLE

In coastal cruising, one often rounds headlands and points which have to be cleared by a certain distance because of off-lying rocks, wrecks, or other dangers. The use of bow and beam bearings, or other methods depending upon the change of bearing of an object on shore, require time spent in plotting and also depend upon an accurate knowledge of the distance made good over the bottom. With any current flowing, this may be quite difficult and the results not too reliable.

If the point or headland is at all high and has an object on it whose location and elevation can accurately be obtained from the chart, the use of the vertical sextant angle is much more certain and less time consuming. A lighthouse on a point is ideal, since the light list will give the exact height of the light and its location.

Draw a circle on the chart around your lighthouse or other object, with a large enough radius to keep you well clear of any obstructions. With the radius of this circle in miles and the height of the object in feet, enter a table of vertical sextant angles and take out the appropriate angle. Table 9 in Bowditch is intended for this purpose, and similar tables are to be found in many almanacs and textbooks on navigation.

Set your sextant to the angle obtained from the table, and keep it close at hand as you approach the headland. An occasional view of the object through the sextant will tell you instantly whether you are within the danger circle. You need not bother about making any adjustments on the sextant—just hold it up to your eye and look. As you see the image of the object begin to approach the horizon, you will know that you are coming up to the danger circle and that you must bear off. If the actual sea horizon is not visible, because of the land mass, use the *dip short of the horizon*, instead of the usual dip correction. This may be taken by inspection from Table 22 in Bowditch.

This method, which is so easy once you run through it a few times, will take you around a rocky point with a constant assurance that you are outside the danger area, and yet without wasting your time by getting unnecessary offing.

TRACING PAPER AS A NAVIGATING INSTRUMENT

The space available on most yachts for charts, navigating instruments, reference books, etc. is relatively limited. At the same time, the basic navigational problems of the offshore yachtsman are not much different from those of the navigator on a merchant ship, and in some instances they require just as much accuracy. One way you can reduce the bulk of your gear is to learn to make use of the versatility of tracing paper. It can be used for a large number of purposes, and any single sheet of it can be used for any one of its many applications.

Get the best quality paper you can find, since it is stronger and less affected by dampness. Buy it in pads or have your stationer make it up into pads in sizes to fit your anticipated uses. I like to carry one pad of 17 inches x 22 inches, one of 8 inches x 11 inches, and one of 5 inches x 7 inches. The smaller sizes could be cut from sheets off a large size pad, but time is important to the yacht skipper who has many things to attend to in addition to the navigation.

I like the sight reduction forms developed by Mixter and shown in his excellent *Primer of Navigation*. Bowditch shows quite adequate work forms in Appendix Q, but they lack the memory aids included in Mixter's forms, and I think these are very important for someone who does not make a full time career of navigating. I often find it difficult to buy the pads of Mixter's forms, however, so I have resorted to keeping one copy of each in my navigating notebook. These are protected with wallpaper lacquer. I clip a sheet of tracing paper over the desired form and do my calculations on the tracing paper. Since I never use the actual forms, I never run out of them.

For celestial navigation off shore, the Series 3000-Oz to 3000-15z Plotting sheets put out by the U.S. Naval Oceanographic Office are ideal. Each sheet covers three degrees of latitude, and the set of 16 sheets covers everything from 49° N. to 49° S. The problem, on a long cruise, is carrying enough sheets of each latitude range to be sure that you will not run out. Again, I have one set of these sheets, lacquered to protect them, and the 17 inch x 22 inch pad of tracing paper. The sixteen sheets take up very little space, and each sheet of tracing paper can be used for any latitude range desired.

If you wish, you can dispense with the plotting sheets altogether, and simply use the tracing paper over any chart which covers the appropriate latitude. Ignore the chart details and use only the Mercator grid and the compass roses. If you do this, always work from the *true* compass rose, since the magnetic variation shown on the chart will not be correct for your plotting.

Whenever you can identify three points on shore, you can establish your position with great accuracy, especially if the points are widely separated. With your sextant, measure the horizontal angles separating these points, and write them down. The only sextant correction is for index error. Take a large sheet of tracing paper, and mark a point somewhere on it to represent your yacht. From this point, draw three lines separated by the angles you have just measured with your sextant. Now go to your chart of the area and locate the three objects which you have used for landmarks. Place the tracing paper over the chart and move it around until the three lines pass through the three points simultaneously. The point where the three lines intersect is the location of your yacht. Prick through the tracing paper to transfer this to the chart.

This method, much more accurate than compass cross-bearings, ordinarily requires the use of a station pointer (large and expensive) or of a special three-armed protractor. The tracing paper does just as well if you are careful in laying off the angles.

You can often locate your position quite accurately by echo sounder when you are on soundings. Check your chart and note the depths at which bottom contours are marked on it. Make a list of these particular depths. Steer in a straight line on a known course while you watch the echo sounder. Each time it reads one of the depths on your list, read the log and enter the log reading oposite the appropriate depth on your list. Continue this for about a mile.

On a sheet of tracing paper, lay off a vertical line to represent a meridian on your chart, and relative to this, draw a line to represent your course. Along the course line, using the distance scale from the chart on which you are plotting, tick off the distances between your recorded log readings. Label each of these with the appropriate depth reading. Now, slide the tracing paper around over the chart, keeping the north-south line parallel to the meridians on the chart, until you see your ticks line up with a series of contour lines on the chart. Check to see if the depths correspond. This will give you your track while the depths were being recorded and your position at the last such recorded depth.

Remember that your log reads distance *through the water,* and that the chart contours are related to the *bottom.* At slack water, this will make no difference, but if a current is running you must make allowance for it, both in the course made good and in the actual distance run between recorded depths. This necessitates careful plotting and reliable current charts, but there are times when one has nothing else on which to rely. I have used it with gratifying results in a fog when large steel bridges in the vicinity made the RDF unreliable.

XI

MISCELLANEOUS

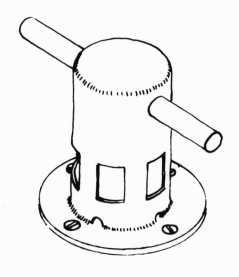

ROLLER REEFING PROCEDURE

One finds, in yachting literature, many excellent step by step directions for tying in a reef with reef points, but the comments on roller reefing are usually limited to a discussion of how simple it is, and the suggestion that one just "rolls in the reef." Somehow I have never found it that simple. Neither have I ever found any great unanimity among yachtsmen as to just how this should be done. Eric Hiscock explains it quite well in *Cruising Under Sail*, but he fails to emphasize the really important point enough for me to have grasped it from his discussion.

After sailing with roller reefing for a number of years on several yachts, I had come to the conclusion that it was practically impossible to roller-reef a mainsail and have it set as well as one in which the reef is tied in with reef points. This was reinforced by the numerous suggestions and remedies I heard of by listening to other yachtsmen. These solutions ranged all the way from attaching specially tapered wooden battens to the boom to inserting pillows and sail bags as the reef is rolled to take up the slack in the sail. Somehow this failed to satisfy me, and I remained convinced that it could be done or it would not be so widely used by such capable racing skippers.

Then I stumbled on a method that works. It is obviously the one that has always been used by all knowledgeable sailing men, but I had always missed the centrally important point. I shall pass it on here, and try to explain the mistakes I had been making.

First, to get a good reef with a roller boom, the sail slides must be free and well oiled, and the track oiler described on page 29 will do that for you. The second requirement for this method of reefing is a worm gear or ratchet such as the Appledore or Turner patterns in England or the well-known Merriman gooseneck in America. Some lighter goosenecks are made so that the boom has to be turned by hand, and these seem to me to be utterly useless, even on a light racing boat. I think you will understand why in a moment.

Go right on sailing while you reef, keeping the sail full and drawing. *Do not round up and let the sail begin to luff*. I think this is the common mistake, and that it is a hang-over from the use of reef points, with which it does no harm to ease the sheet and makes it much easier to haul down the tack and clew as well as to tie in the first two or three points. I think this error may also come from the widespread use of goosenecks which do not have a powerful enough roller mechanism to enable one to roll the boom with the sail filled.

Do not use the topping lift, but let the sail support the boom as you reef. By bringing the halyard down to the pin rail and under a pin, I can ease it with one hand while turning the roller crank with the other. If there is no place for you to snub the halyard, you may have to have someone else ease it out as you turn the boom. At any rate, ease the halyard *just* enough to keep up with the rolling of the boom. Never allow the luff to become slack. The tight luff and the wind in the sail will support the weight of the boom, and the reef will roll in smoothly and with little or no tendency to wrinkle.

Roll the reef down to the point where the yacht sails easily again, and then belay the halyard. Now roll the boom just enough more to set up the luff perfectly taut. On a large boat, one cannot haul hard enough on the halyard to tighten the luff with the sail drawing, but you can do it easily this way. The weight of the boom and sail works for you rather than against you, and the tremendous power of the worm gear gives you perfect control.

If you carry a trysail, you will probably never reef beyond the second batten of your mainsail. Below this point, the leach of the sail takes a terrible stretching from the weight of the boom and the pull of the sheets. However, you will often reef beyond the first, or lowest batten. Therefore, if the lower batten pocket is not parallel to the boom, take your sail to the sailmaker and have him change it. Then you can roll the batten right into the reef, and if you have ever tried to get a batten out of a sail in a high wind when the yacht is being tossed around by heavy seas, you will appreciate the desirability of this.

Now, where had I been going wrong? In the first place, I had been rounding up and letting most of the wind out of the sail—not enough to let it flog, but enough to take most of the strain off the halyard. Of course, this meant that the boom had to be supported by the topping lift, and this in turn meant that the sail was not stretched nice and tight as it rolled onto the boom. It will roll on smoothly if you give it a chance, but this means you have to allow the weight of the boom and the force of the wind to keep it stretched tightly and to distribute the tension evenly.

It sounds extremely simple, doesn't it? It is, too, but having missed the extreme importance of what seems to be the really basic point in the procedure, I was a long time in seeing the light.

ABANDONING SHIP

This is a subject all of us would prefer not to think about. It is very seldom called for, but if it should ever become necessary, a little forethought and planning may well make the difference between surviving and not surviving. I am sure that the best general advice that can be given about abandoning a yacht is *don't do it if you can possibly avoid it.* Are you really bettering your situation by leaving the yacht? Unless it is burning or sinking out from under you, your yacht will give you a better chance of survival than a life raft. It should go without saying that almost *anything* is better than abandoning your yacht in your dinghy. Most yacht dinghies are not too seaworthy in a sheltered harbor, and they'll not last five minutes in sea conditions that threaten the yacht itself.

If one accepts this, what provisions should one make for the possibility of having to abandon the yacht at sea? The approved, self-inflating rubber life rafts seem to be the best answer, and by all means get one which *contains* a survival kit. If you ever do have to abandon your yacht, you may not have time to gather together the things that you would like to take with you. Mount the raft on deck in an unobstructed position from which you will have some chance of getting it into the water if you need it. Do not stow it below decks to protect it from the sun and weather.

The survival kit contained in the life raft will provide emergency rations, fishing tackle, flares and smoke signals, a knife, and some fresh water. It would seem wise, before beginning a long passage, to make up an emergency pack to supplement these supplies. It should contain a flare pistol and at least three boxes of red flare cartridges, six or more colored smoke signals, three light wool blankets, a ball of marline, an inexpensive pair of binoculars or field glasses, a waterproof flashlight with spare batteries and bulbs, a jar of zinc oxide ointment, and as much fresh water as you feel you can practically stow. I would suggest that two gallons of fresh water in one quart plastic bottles is about all you can afford to carry.

Pack this gear in plastic bags and enclose it in one large heavy plastic bag. Pack this inside a canvas bag such as a sail bag, and stow the kit on deck by the life raft. Have a line attached to the kit so you can make it fast to the raft after it has been launched. Appoint some particular member of the crew to open the kit once a month, wash out the water bottles, refill them, and repack the kit.

What should your goals be, if you have to leave the yacht, and you find yourself and your crew afloat in the inflated raft watching the yacht go down? First of all, accept the fact that you are not going to go anywhere. If you are only a few miles offshore with a favorable wind, you might be realistic if you start paddling. Otherwise your two considerations must be for staying alive and attracting the attention of a passing ship or airplane. If you keep in mind that these are the *only* two things that matter, some intelligent plans can be made to increase your chances.

Once you are aboard the raft and free from the yacht, see to it that each man is attached to the raft by a safety line. They need not be very long, as there is not much space for moving around, but falling or being washed overboard is a constant danger and this factor will increase as time goes by and you become more fatigued and less alert.

If your raft has a self-contained shelter over it, and it should have, this will help to keep off the sun during the day, as well as protecting you from wind and water. If no such "tent" is included with the raft, rig one from one of the blankets and the oars for the raft. The more shelter you get from the sun and wind, the less water you will require. Use the zinc oxide ointment liberally on your hands and face to *prevent* sunburn, and insist that everyone keep his shirt on during the heat of the day. A severe case of sunburn will not make things any easier for any of you and the fever that may accompany it will increase the need for water.

Don't try to get dry until the sea conditions are such that you can hope to *stay* dry for a while. If you open the emergency pack for the dry blankets in the midst of a real storm, they will be soaked in a matter of seconds. When things have calmed down a bit, get the raft bailed out and then remove and dry all the wet clothing. Try to keep one or two of the blankets dry and wrapped in plastic, so you will be able to use them later if another storm blows up.

Put a marline lanyard on *each* piece of gear and insist that they be kept tied to the raft. If each man and article is attached to the raft, even if you should capsize completely as you well may in a bad sea, there will be a chance of getting everyone and everything back aboard again.

Set up a strict water rationing immediately. Each man should be able to survive for some time on less than a pint of water a day. Keep the raft bailed out dry so that any rain which does fall into it will be drinkable. Don't worry too much about the food. You can last quite a time without food if you do not exert yourself too much, and you may be able to catch some fish with the gear in your kit.

Set some watches immediately, and keep using the binoculars. Your only real hope lies in spotting and signalling a ship, so don't miss any chances. When you do see a ship, try to determine its course as soon as possible. Your action will now depend upon your position. If you are within or near regular shipping lanes, you can expect to see a fair number of ships. In this case, don't waste any of your smoke signals or flares on a ship that is not likely to see you. Wait until one comes close enough to make a sighting likely, and then set off your signals.

Most merchant ships keep their most vigilant look-out toward their own danger zone. If you see a ship approaching, try to determine if it will pass you so that your raft will be on the ship's starboard bow. If so, wait until you are in this sector and then set off your fireworks. Even if the ship appears to sight you and starts to approach, keep the smoke signals going from time to time. A small life raft is not an easy thing to keep in view from any distance, so give the ship something to go by. At night, continue to fire a flare now and then and keep your flashlight pointed at the ship's bridge. If the ship approaches at night, she will probably signal with an Aldis lamp. *If you know Morse code well,* answer the signal with your flashlight. If you do not, ignore the signalling and just keep your light directed at the ship's bridge. Any half-correct or improvised signalling on your part will only confuse the signalman on the ship.

If you have had to abandon your yacht well outside the shipping lanes, the situation is somewhat different. You may not see a ship for several days, and when you do you must make the most of it since you can't be sure when another will come along. In this case, you will have to gamble on a long shot and start using your signals as soon as there is any likelihood of their being seen. Your best chance will be in the late evening. A flare can be seen from a long distance, and at this time of day some of the off-duty crew may be on deck so you'll not have to rely entirely on the watch to see your signals. Flares are not very impressive when it is not dark, so rely on the smoke signals during the daylight hours.

One sometimes feels that carrying an umbrella helps to guarantee a nice sunny day. At least if it does rain, one can open the umbrella. As unpleasant as this subject of survival at sea may be, some advance consideration and preparation could well enable you to tell the story to your grandchildren.

APPENDIX

Most Americans and some Englishmen still labor under the delusion that the two countries share a common language. This fallacy is compounded by the fact that each *can* understand *most* of what the other says in casual conversation. In technical areas, however, the terms are often quite different, and I have prepared this short list of the more important differences and equivalents in the nautical vocabularies of the two countries. I have not included minor and regular differences in spelling, such as *miter* and *mitre, harbor* and *harbour,* etc., since these present no barrier to understanding.

I have sailed for several years, now, on English yachts and with English yachtsmen, and I find that I am no longer able to distinguish with complete certainty between the two sets of terms. I hope that the list that follows will serve to make the text of this book at least legible if not palatable to both American and English readers.

American	*English*
jibe	gybe
turnbuckle	rigging screw or bottle screw
spreaders	cross trees
fore staysail	often foresail
fender	fend-off
drafting	draughting
triangles	set-squares
kerosene	paraffin
lamp cord	flex
stove	cooker
toilet	water closet (W.C.)
closet	cupboard
plastic sheeting	p.v.c. sheet
tube (radio)	valve
radio	wireless
generator	dynamo
battery	accumulator
antenna	aerial
ground (elec.)	earth

spark plug	sparking plug
spacer	distance piece
bushing	bush
wrench	spanner
muffler	silencer
truck	lorry
tire	tyre
four-cycle	four-stroke
Dacron	terylene
Lucite or Plexiglass	Perspex
clothespin	clothespeg

The size of *wire* rope is expressed in both countries as the measurement of the diameter. Fibre rope, on the other hand, is described in terms of its *diameter* in America but in terms of its *circumference* in England.

Remember too, that the British measures of volume or capacity are not equivalent to the American measures, even though they bear the same names. For example, the British Imperial Gallon is equal to 1.2 American gallons—almost equivalent to five U. S. quarts. This is enough to make quite a difference in fuel consumption calculations, so bear it in mind if you are considering an English engine. When its manufacturers talk about a gallon of fuel, they mean a British gallon.

We Americans say we use the "English" system of measurements, when we are talking about feet and inches as opposed to meters and centimeters. It is not very widely known that the American foot and the English foot are not the same size. Admittedly, the difference is extremely small—one U. S. foot equals 1.00000373 British feet, but nevertheless it does officially exist. Perhaps this is just another valid argument for the universal adoption of the metric system.